More Praise for *Managing Projects*

"Successfully managing projects takes more than good task- and time-management skills. In *Managing Projects*, Lou Russell discusses the all-important role that influencing plays in getting things done—on time, on spec, and on budget—and weaves this into a rock-solid walkthrough of the principal steps of a project. This is a must-read for anyone with project responsibility—in other words, everyone."

— Martin Delahoussaye, vice president publishing, HRDQ

"The book converts the usually boring and intimidating world of project management into easy steps and practical approaches. The ideas are useful and immediately applicable."

— Ray Jimenez, PhD, Vignettes Learning

"Lou Russell is the perfect expert on project management productivity and engagement to write this substantive book. Whether you are a fledgling project manager or a twenty-year veteran, this book will give you the tools to help you manage through constraints and communication. I highly recommend her work."

— Teresa Conroy-Roth, senior vice president, Technology Partnership Group, Inc.

"Workload, complexity, and pressure have increased dramatically. For companies to achieve their strategic goals all staff must be competent in basic project management. Lou's book provides just enough to build a baseline but not so much that it overwhelms."

— Jane Niederberger, former senior vice president and chief information officer, Anthem Inc.; former vice president operations, WellPoint; investor and consultant, Healthcare Technology and Operations, Neiderberger Ventures, Inc.

"Anyone who feels overloaded and distracted will benefit from Lou's new book, *Managing Projects*. Lou's book provides hands-on tools to sort through the complexity of a work world that is constantly changing and understaffed. Today's world requires different project-management skills than even five years ago. Thank you, Lou, for this easy-to-read update!"

— Karen Valencic, Spiral Impact

"In *Managing Projects*, Lou Russell takes you through a practical journey of immediate project management implementation. She structured the book in a unique fashion, in which I was able to learn, reflect, and implement the principles of project management then and there. Very useful and clever."

— Maha Khatib, principal, Learnactive, Dubai

"If it suddenly seems like you are in charge of *everything* and even multitasking at the speed of light isn't cutting through the chaos, Lou's book helps you rein in the madness and complete more projects with less help, time, and money. You'll learn how to give up control and actually start managing things so you can finally end the day feeling like you've accomplished something."
— **Leah Nelson, senior conference program manager, *Training* magazine Events**

"Among those things you can count on are death, taxes, and Lou Russell's ability to transform complex ideas into interesting and immediately usable insights. *Managing Projects* is yet another example of Lou's gift of making even the most mundane and tedious aspects of project management a captivating and enlightening read. If you spend any of your time trying to run a project you'd be crazy not to invest the time in reading this book."
— **Dan Brandon, associate director, Financial Services Industry**

"Lou Russell demystifies project management with simple yet incredibly effective steps and tools that any project manager can understand and use. Lou provides a good dose of team building to the process that gets everyone on board … and in most cases that has been the missing element."
— **Deb George, The Children's Museum of Indianapolis**

"This book should be titled *The Missing Links of Managing Projects.* From her deep understanding and project management experience, Lou Russell shares unique insights on often overlooked yet highly critical issues that greatly impact the outcomes of our initiatives. An essential volume that will benefit project managers at every level."
— **Gary VanAntwerp, vice president, Implementation, *Training* magazine Network, SMMConnect, VFTNetworks**

"In Chapter One of *Managing Projects*, Lou Russell contends that 'project management is … a required competency for all business workers.' I couldn't agree more, and there is no greater blessing to the full-time, professional project manager than leading a team made up of individuals with an understanding and competency in project management. Lou's accessible approach to project management makes that ideal closer to reality."
— **Kevin Weston, vice president, IT Planning, OneAmerica companies**

"*Managing Projects* is a practical and relevant book for anyone engaged in today's crazy work world. Lou describes the situation facing us so accurately I felt like she must have been following me around! Finally, I now have a guide to help me manage the chaos and feel good about myself in the process."
— **Lori Miller, alumna, Lou's Project Management certificate program**

ABOUT THIS BOOK

WHY IS THIS BOOK IMPORTANT?

There are three forces combining to create an unmanageable workload and work life for people: staffing, technology, and fear. Reduced staff in the workplace means that most people are asked to juggle multiple jobs that were previously done by other people. People are universally juggling multiple projects while playing multiple roles, all while doing their real job. Technology helps us work more quickly, but it follows us 24/7, triggering constant interruption and driving inefficient multitasking. Fear is rampant because layoffs are continuing, and it is evident that each of us can only scale so far before we break. Fear drives stress, which drives poor-quality projects. This book helps clarify how these three factors drive unreasonable project expectations, poor quality, and constant rework, which in turn increases fear. It's a negative reinforcing loop. To escape this new triple constraint requires that we bite the bullet and change the way we do projects.

WHAT CAN YOU ACHIEVE WITH THIS BOOK?

First, this book challenges the way you look at your workload. You will learn quick, simple ways to work on the most important projects while keeping your interruptions at bay. Next, this book helps you communicate with others more effectively through a 30-minute Project Charter, creating realistic expectations when a project starts and facilitating bad news early—when you can still do something about it. Then, as you plan and manage each of your projects, you'll learn how to influence others and manage yourself so that the stress doesn't destroy your ability to adapt. Finally, you'll learn how to take small bits of time to capture lessons learned and grow your own ability to manage a flexible structure on every project. Best of all, at least a couple of times a week, you will leave work feeling like you actually accomplished something.

HOW IS THIS BOOK ORGANIZED?

You can approach this book in different ways. If you are on a project right now and you have a specific question about how to manage a particular issue, you can skip right to Chapters 2 (Define), 3 (Plan), 4 (Manage), or 5 (Review) and find tools and techniques that are immediately applicable. If you are new to project management, focus on Chapters 2–5 for a primer that gets you through the entire project management process. Do a project while reading these chapters for maximum value. If you are a more experienced project manager, consider skimming Chapters 2–5 and focusing on Chapters 6–7 to grow your ability to manage a portfolio of projects for your organization. Finally, Chapter 8 is designed to celebrate your success and review the whole book. You can start there if you'd like, wait until the end, or save it for a rainy day.

About Pfeiffer

Pfeiffer serves the professional development and hands-on resource needs of training and human resource practitioners and gives them products to do their jobs better. We deliver proven ideas and solutions from experts in HR development and HR management, and we offer effective and customizable tools to improve workplace performance. From novice to seasoned professional, Pfeiffer is the source you can trust to make yourself and your organization more successful.

Essential Knowledge Pfeiffer produces insightful, practical, and comprehensive materials on topics that matter the most to training and HR professionals. Our Essential Knowledge resources translate the expertise of seasoned professionals into practical, how-to guidance on critical workplace issues and problems. These resources are supported by case studies, worksheets, and job aids and are frequently supplemented with CD-ROMs, websites, and other means of making the content easier to read, understand, and use.

Essential Tools Pfeiffer's Essential Tools resources save time and expense by offering proven, ready-to-use materials—including exercises, activities, games, instruments, and assessments—for use during a training or team-learning event. These resources are frequently offered in looseleaf or CD-ROM format to facilitate copying and customization of the material.

Pfeiffer also recognizes the remarkable power of new technologies in expanding the reach and effectiveness of training. While e-hype has often created whizbang solutions in search of a problem, we are dedicated to bringing convenience and enhancements to proven training solutions. All our e-tools comply with rigorous functionality standards. The most appropriate technology wrapped around essential content yields the perfect solution for today's on-the-go trainers and human resource professionals.

Essential resources for training and HR professionals

www.pfeiffer.com

Managing Projects

A Practical Guide for Learning Professionals

Lou Russell
President, Russell Martin & Associates

Pfeiffer

A Wiley Imprint
www.pfeiffer.com

Published by Pfeiffer
An Imprint of Wiley
One Montgomery Street, Suite 1200, San Francisco, CA 94104-4594—www.pfeiffer.com

Pfeiffer books and products are available through most bookstores. To contact Pfeiffer directly call our Customer Care Department within the U.S. at 800-274-4434, outside the U.S. at 317-572-3985, fax 317-572-4002, or visit www.pfeiffer.com.

Pfeiffer publishes in a variety of print and electronic formats and by print-on-demand. Some material included with standard print versions of this book may not be included in e-books or in print-on-demand. If this book refers to media such as a CD or DVD that is not included in the version you purchased, you may download this material at http://booksupport.wiley.com. For more information about Wiley products, visit www.wiley.com.

Acquiring Editor: Matthew Davis
Production Editor: Robin Stephanie Lloyd
Editor: Jeffrey Wyneken
Editorial Assistant: Michael Zelenko
Manufacturing Supervisor: Becky Morgan

Library of Congress Cataloging-in-Publication Data
Russell, Lou, 1957-
   Managing projects : a practical guide for learning professionals /
Lou Russell. - 1st ed.
        p. cm.
   Includes index.
   ISBN 978-1-118-02203-0 (pbk.)
   ISBN 978-1-118-28214-4 (ebk.)
   ISBN 978-1-118-28298-4 (ebk.)
   ISBN 978-1-118-28433-9 (ebk.)
   1. Project management. I. Title.
   HD69.P75R873 2012
   658.4′04-dc23
                                                                    2012003659

Printed in the United States of America
FIRST EDITION

PB Printing 10 9 8 7 6 5 4 3 2 1

CONTENTS

LIST OF EXHIBITS

PREFACE

I am a shiny object person. I really like working on new things, and I'm not very good at finishing things up, including this book (special thanks to Matt Holt, Pfeiffer acquisition editor extraordinaire, for his infinite patience). I consider myself a very creative person, and love discussing new ideas. It became evident to me as I started my own consulting business over 25 years ago that I was going to have to figure out a discipline that would help me successfully juggle and finish multiple projects.

As a beginning programmer at AT&T in the late 1970s, I had project management procedures (they were called BSPs, for Bell Systems Practices) that were so detailed they specified how many wastebaskets and ashtrays you would need for your project. Times have seriously changed. In those days, projects were done by dedicated teams with one dedicated project manager. Today, I am juggling multiple projects (not unlike you, I'm sure) with a highly matrixed group of stakeholders, most of whom do not report to me in any formal capacity.

That's not the only thing that has changed since my days at AT&T. For example, I once worked on a project where I was told to first research the requirements and then, when I was all finished, to tell the business area the project was done. In others words, I had all the time I needed, no matter what happened along the way. Today, I might get a call with a brief description of the project and a due date; I work backward, not forward.

The project management methods and techniques you will read about in this book reflect the "I need it now" nature of the world you and I live in. We don't have time for 100 pages of proper project management process. We need to be adaptable and agile. Every day we must be prepared to completely adapt to new or changing needs. This book represents what I believe to be an easier and more realistic way to approach project management.

I have arranged the book in two parts. The first part (Chapters 1–5) provides all the techniques you need to define, plan, manage, and review a project. The second part (Chapters 6–8) shows you how to manage the people side of a project, including how to deal with change and its impact on others in your organization; and how to influence unruly stakeholders and create organizational dashboards.

HARD AND SOFT SKILLS IN ONE BOOK

One of the most exciting aspects of this book is that it is really two books in one. For the first time, I am able to offer you two sets of skills: the "hard skills" of following a project management process in order to successfully manage your project; and at the same time, the "soft skills" (which are often "harder"!) of managing the people who participate in a project as well as those who are impacted by it.

I hope that you will use this book not only to manage your projects more efficiently so that you save both time and money, but also to improve the quality of your life. After all, you and likely everyone you know are working far too many hours under far too much stress. Many employees feel they are being held hostage to their job. Perhaps your being smarter about how you manage projects will help your organization see you as the valuable asset you really are. Use these techniques then to take care of yourself and your family. As I like to say to those who take my classes, "Insanity is just a project constraint." You shouldn't take any of what goes on around you too personally; just learn to adapt, laugh, and move on.

Special thanks to my family for their support in everything I do. Thanks to my husband, Doug, for rushing to the store and buying me a new power cable for my laptop when I left one in New Jersey. I just left the new one in Minnesota as well … sigh. He tries very hard to take care of me, but the shiny objects can still attract me and are my undoing.

Special thanks to my beautiful and talented daughters, Kelly, Kristin, and Katherine. Kelly has graduated and has a real job, and is learning her own project management. It's fun to watch. Kristin and Katherine are juggling academics and sports like pros. I'm proud of them all.

Thanks also to Brittney Tiemann, my project manager, business development manager, and at the moment my whole staff. She was a miracle find after the recession rebooted my business, and I owe a lot to her.

Thanks to Mark Morrow, the "msfixer," who helped me stay true to my voice. And thanks to all the students who have helped me evolve these ideas and taught me much more than I have taught them.

LET'S GET GOING

In this book, I share a simple, visual, and practical way to manage your projects. I also share some ideas with you at the end of the book for joining with others in your organization to adopt a project management approach together. In these tough times, a business cannot survive unless its limited resources (and you are one of these) are aligned with the most important work. The chapters ahead will help you do the following:

Chapter 2: Define

Why is the enterprise spending money on my project instead of something else?

Chapter 3: Plan

How are we going to get this project done?

Chapter 4: Manage

Adapt to the project reality

Chapter 5: Review

Learn how to improve project management capacity

Chapter 6: Organizational Change

Navigate the pushback as your project introduces a New World

Chapter 7: Organizational Project Management

Grow a repeatable process for project management and establishing project mentoring

Chapter 8: Insanity Is Just a Project Constraint

Now that you're organized, how will you stay that way?

You can certainly use this book as a reference guide, jumping to a tool you need in a project emergency. I'd recommend a different approach if you are expecting to get lasting improvement from this book. This is a real *hands-on* book that gives you the opportunity to learn while you do. So, if you'd like to "jump right in," then I'd suggest reading Chapters 2 and 3 and trying the techniques on a project you're currently working on. Then read Chapter 4 right before you kick off the project. Read Chapter 5 just as you are finishing up the project.

Chapter 6 will help you when your project stakeholders are driving you crazy—I mean to the point where you want to throw up your hands because you just "don't think you can stand it anymore." Reading this chapter will help you put these stakeholders' behavior in perspective and see their behavior as admittedly irritating but actually very normal. This shift in attitude and mindset will help you react more effectively and reduce your stress level.

Chapter 7 is designed to help you create a common language and shared process/documentation strategy. I provide this information because once everyone in your organization notices that your projects are a lot more organized than everyone else's, you are likely to be very popular. So this chapter sets you up to become the project management guru of sorts.

Chapter 8 is my final shot at encouraging you to take your life back. Maybe put a Post-it at the start of this brief chapter so you can read it whenever you're feeling overwhelmed. It will give you a little laugh and get you back into the trenches. It's all about adapting.

ADVICE AT THE START

Think about major changes you had to make in your life, such as choosing to have children, getting married, or changing jobs. Each transition made you nervous about the decision but excited about how it would improve your life. In most cases (I hope), your life was improved a great deal, transformed forever, in fact. However, making these changes was not easy and was likely full of bumps, dragons, surprises, insanity, and trials and tribulations. Still, the blessings and opportunities you received were almost always worth the bumpy and often frightening ride.

You will likely face the same dynamic as you take this step to improve your ability to manage projects.

Think about how many times you leave work frustrated that you were unable to finish the things you'd planned to get done that day. Even worse, you discover that the day has added new things to your list, which was already too long. Each day may just seem impossible. Relax. You are not alone. Here are some recent frustrations shared by my workshop students:

- It seems impossible to check anything off. There is always some part of a project or task that's not quite done or a person who hasn't done what they said they would do. Everything on the list seems to stay an open issue forever.

- Email, social media, and all digital communication are overwhelming. It takes hours each day to keep from drowning entirely under the weight of all the help others need from you.

- No one helps. Worse, no one does what they say they'd do or promised, and no one delivers anything when they said they would deliver it.

- There is no time to be strategic. All I seem to do is put out "fires."

- There aren't enough people to do the work, so I am currently juggling the project workload of multiple people. It's hard to keep it all straight when I'm constantly jumping between projects, and I'm usually doing this juggling act through emails.

- If I make a fuss, I'll be the first name on the next layoff list.

- I've compromised my health and sacrificed time with my family to juggle this insane workload.

- I am past being scalable. I am painfully aware of the lack of quality in my work and I'm drowning in the rework caused by all this juggling.

This list may express the pain that prompted you to open this book. If not, make a note in the margin of what you'd like to change in your workload and life. Life is what good project management is all about. If we can prioritize and manage the important things while saying no to the less important things, we can have success, and so can the businesses we work for.

September 2011   LOU RUSSELL

CHAPTER 1

Start Well to End Well

"Bad News early is Good News."   — Steve McNamara

In this chapter:

- How to really do more (projects) with less (help, money, time)
- Why project management is not too hard or academic for you to use every day
- Using PMI's methodologies and other project management methods
- How to feel like you've accomplished something at the end of each day
- How to stop trying to *control* and start *managing*
- How to establish the partnerships required for projects to be successful

In today's chaotic business climate, multitasking is the norm. Jobs have been trimmed, and companies are doing more with less. Roles and responsibilities cannot be defined clearly enough to adapt to the work responsibilities required to flex with the chaos. No one is accountable, except you of course. People are juggling multiple projects and often acting as the project manager for a team of one.

 Lou's Project Management Diary

As part of a recent study conducted by Towers Perrin and the researchers of Gang & Gang, a randomly selected group of 1,100 employees and 300 senior human resource executives working for midsized and large-sized companies in the United States and Canada was surveyed. Participants were asked to describe their feelings about their current work. The study captured participants' spontaneous emotional responses about the total work experience. The study determined a set of reasons for workplace negativity. Here are the top five:

- An excessive workload
- Concerns about management's ability to lead the company forward successfully
- Anxiety about the future, particularly longer-term jobs, income, and retirement security
- Lack of challenge in their work; boredom that intensifies existing frustration about workload
- Insufficient recognition (including salary) for performance, contribution, and effort

Think about a project that you are on right now. Use Sidebar 1.1 to think about your project experiences.

The negative emotion is an uncomfortable place in your mind, but I'd like you to stay there for a moment so you can learn more about your current project management competence. If you are like many of my learners, you have written down the word "frustration" or "stress," or something like that. Overall, 80 percent of the learners in our classes list one of these two words when they do this exercise. As a mini-snapshot of current work, the thought that 80 percent of workers are stressed out is not a positive sign. When we are in an almost constant state of frustration, we don't make good decisions, and our projects struggle.

Let's look at some of the other potential triggers. Your list may include:

- People who aren't accountable
- People who won't deliver on or meet their promised deadlines
- Not enough time
- No executive support
- Unreasonable budgets
- Internal political battles that have nothing to do with the project
- Stakeholders continually changing the scope of the project
- No help

Then, many of our students share the impact of this emotional state on their personal life. These impacts include:

- Limited time and energy for families
- Health issues
- The threat of unemployment due to project failure

In this book, you will learn how to respond to these triggers with preemptive strikes. You will also learn how to recognize when you're lying to yourself, thus creating some of the very stress-inducing triggers you blame on others. Project success through good project management is all about communication with yourself and others. Projects break down during phase transitions and hand-offs—and in large measure due to self-deception.

Return to the positive emotion you wrote about in Sidebar 1.1. The positive emotions tend to be more diverse, which makes sense because what motivates individuals varies greatly. Notice what motivates you and keep it in mind for when your projects head to the negative side.

A BRIEF HISTORY OF PROJECT MANAGEMENT

Work has changed and accelerated, contributing to our feelings of stress and frustration. How many times a week do you leave work overwhelmed? Or put another way, how many times a week do you never leave work—even if you physically leave the office? Today's technology allows work to follow us 24/7, wherever we go, nagging us about all we've left unfinished.

Gone are the days when you, along with a team of people, were dedicated to a single project. Sure, you may have had your day-to-day job responsibilities, but you were able to focus many hours a day on one single project. Handing off or transitioning between project phases was easier because the other people on your team were also dedicated to your single project. Today, most people are juggling multiple projects at a time. Whenever you need something from someone else, you might be interrupting them at work on another project or, in our digitally connected world, sorting through their email. A recent statistic claimed that workers on average spend half of their day processing emails. My theory is that 75 percent of that time is spent trying to frantically delete, save, or somehow get rid of emails, not actually processing something important.

Project management, which realistically has been around since the Egyptians built the pyramids (at least!), became an official practice in 1969 with the beginning of the Project Management Institute in the United States, known as PMI (www.pmi.org). This international not-for-profit association researches and establishes best practices in project management. The collection of best practices is called the Project Management Body of Knowledge, or PMBOK for short (pronounced as a word, *pimbok*). PMI also offers an increasing number of certification programs, including the Project Management Professional (PMP pronounced as letters, for obvious reasons) certification, which requires extensive project work, training, and a rigorous written test. PMPs must attend training and development programs to keep their certification as well. Your local PMI organization is a good resource for inexpensive, quality training and the place to go if you would like to be a certified project manager.

Many of the techniques and processes in the PMBOK assume that a project manager is a dedicated specialist. Due to the complexity of technology and work, I believe project management is no longer just for specialists but a required competency for all business workers. Learning project management as a competency is different from project management as a specialty, profession, and full-time job. This book will focus on the competency of project management as opposed to the career.

In addition, traditional project management starts with the project manager building the due date using a detailed project plan, a process I will refer to as "going forward." In a sense, the professional project manager is calculating when this project will be done. I believe most of us are "working backwards"; in other words, we are working back from a fixed date and/or budget. You will learn more about this important difference when you get to Chapter 3, on planning the project.

If you are a PMP-certified project manager, this book will add value to your knowledge by providing you with simple techniques that may help you influence your stakeholders and sponsors more effectively. If you are not a PMP, you will acquire a process and simple techniques that will increase your work capacity, augment your project success, and perhaps more important, improve your state of mind. The ideas in this book are completely consistent with PMI's PMBOK, although some of the terminology has been simplified to appeal to this book's audience.

No matter what your background, this book will give you practical, effective project management techniques and tips, especially if you are juggling multiple, smaller projects. If you are managing a large global or multidepartmental project, these techniques will not be sufficient but may be used as a starting point. Still, most readers will be able to apply these techniques to manage their own portfolio of projects, which are often done with temporary help and driven by aggressive timelines and limited budgets.

WHAT IS A PROJECT?

I've already mentioned the current state of work and the increasing levels of complexity.

Now, let's try another exercise to see why you may be frustrated. Grab another piece of paper and give yourself no more than two minutes to write down what's on your to-do list right now. Write down at least five things but no more than ten. Notice the emotions this list generates and how it impacts your sense of self. Next, refer to Sidebar 1.2.

Let's look at your results and consider the following point. In David Allen's popular book *Getting Things Done,* he says that the reason we make so little progress checking things off our to-do list each day is that we are mixing up projects and tasks.

First, let's look at any items on your list that do not have a *P.* These are likely tasks. What then is a task?

- Tasks have a beginning and end that are clear and measurable

- Tasks can be done by one person

- Tasks can be done in less than four hours, assuming no interruptions

  Examples of tasks might be:

- Complete my timesheet

- Send an email

- Print an invoice

  Think about why the following are not tasks:

- Get a signature of approval

- Hold a meeting

- Implement world peace

The approval signature requires someone else's help. If everything goes perfectly, you will get that signature quickly. But it is more likely that you will have to ask multiple times for the signature to be completed. Having multiple tasks means it's a project. Obviously, you don't need a project plan to get a signature in most cases, but it's important to note that many of the things we think we can check off quickly because they are tasks take longer when other people are involved—lots longer!

"Hold a meeting" is the kind of task that complicates our to-do list. It certainly seems like a task that is straightforward and easy to do. However, holding a meeting actually takes multiple steps and multiple people to make it happen. You might find the room that you need is reserved by your CEO—no negotiation there. Then, you discover that food is not allowed in the only other available room and you are planning a breakfast meeting; or a key stakeholder would like you to move the meeting forward 15 minutes. You see where I'm going. Holding a meeting involves steps and responsibility hand-offs, and is clearly more a project than a task if viewed through a project management lens. It's a project made up of a collection of tasks each with a beginning and end.

I'm guessing you did not put "Implement world peace" on your list, but for a little fun I'll use this as an example of a task (or project) that is difficult to end. How would you or anyone else measure the end point of the project World Peace? Without clear and measurable criteria for "ending," projects will struggle and frustration will grow. In Chapter 2, you will learn how to start a project with clarity and avoid some of these issues.

Simply put, tasks are the smallest unit of work. Many of you may not have *any* tasks on your list! It's easy to check off tasks on your to-do list. It takes a lot longer to complete a project and thus have the satisfaction of checking it off. You know this feeling, I'm sure. That awful feeling at the end of the day that you haven't gotten anything done; in fact, your list is longer than at the start of the day.

Projects are made up of tasks. Most likely you have multiple items attached to the letter *P* in your list. What is a project?

- Projects also have a beginning and end, but either or both can get confusing
- Projects are temporary, and require temporary help from others
- Projects almost always need more than one person's help
- Projects take more than a half day to complete
- Projects add new value to your organization
  Examples of projects might be:
- Design a marketing piece
- Deploy a new performance management system
- Complete a payroll cycle
  Think about why the following are not tasks:
- Offer training
- Do payroll

WHAT IS A PROCESS?

Look at your list again. Some of the items on your list may not have a beginning point or an end point. In fact, we may want to continue these items for an indefinite amount of time; for example, being able to do the payroll indefinitely means your business has long-term viability. What is a process?

- Processes do not really have a beginning and end; they occur repeatedly

- Processes are often permanent, and usually have permanent staff

  A process is also made up of tasks. Think of it this way:

- Doing payroll is a process. A payroll cycle is a project. Printing a payroll check is a task.

- Offering training multiple times requires a process. The collection of tasks to hold a workshop is a project. Printing materials for the workshop might be a task.

The difference between *process*, *project*, and *task* often causes confusion about the scope of a project. For example, what if your organization is implementing a new software package to manage the learning function (these are generally called Learning Management Systems, or LMS). It will take a *project* to choose an LMS and to properly install it and train its users. It will take a *process* to maintain it, update it, and keep it functional after the project of deploying ends. Many people confuse *process* with the maintenance of what gets created and implemented as a result of a project's end product.

Notice that our software project above is actually multiple small projects, often called subprojects. For example, this project might require:

- Selecting the best LMS to purchase

- Installing the LMS

- Establishing processes for using the LMS

- Training people on how to use the LMS

All of these subprojects must be successful for the whole project to be successful. This coordination of multiple large efforts is one of the reasons projects struggle. It's complex, chaotic, and hard to do. In this book, you will learn ways to handle multiple but dependent projects like these.

Some of our clients define *project* in a slightly broader manner, specifically to determine when more formal project status reporting is required. For example, a project might be defined as anything five months long or longer, or as any effort that requires more than $50,000 in a budget. Personally, I try to stay with the "four-hour uninterrupted" criterion (shared at the start of this chapter), keeping a list of projects separate from my list of tasks. You can call this list your "project portfolio." It's likely that you will have projects on your list that vary in size, complexity, and budget, just like a financial portfolio. In Chapter 2 ("Define") you will learn how to prioritize your project work (and your portfolio) based on the risk of the projects.

Another factor that may be driving up your stress levels as you struggle to check things off your list is the hours in a day. Given your normal workday, how many hours in a day can you actually work on projects? If you are like my students, most of you will say no more than two hours (some will say zero!). That means a task that takes four hours to complete will actually take you two days. This is a common point of confusion in project management. Often we confuse and miscalculate the difference between *effort* (the amount of time it will take to complete something uninterrupted) and *duration* (the time that will elapse before we can get enough time to get it done). If you only get two hours a day to work on projects, an *effort* of four hours will take you two days' *duration* to complete.

Take a look back at your to-do list. To improve your feelings of accomplishment at the end of the day, consider doing the following:

- Take projects off your list and replace them with the next one or two tasks that are needed for the project. I will help you figure out what those tasks are in Chapter 2 ("Define") and Chapter 3 ("Plan"). Keep a different list for projects to monitor the status of. More on that in Chapter 4 ("Manage").

- Take processes off your list and replace them with the tasks of the current project/cycle; for example, a payroll cycle. You'll add this project to your project list and manage the tasks like above.

- Start each day with a list of tasks to accomplish by estimating how long it will take to do each one and then mapping that to the number of hours you can work on projects in a day. Obviously, it makes no sense to expect to finish ten hours of tasks when you can only do two hours of project work a day.

- Work on increasing the amount of time you can work on projects each day by learning to say no and managing your email more effectively.

- Most important, tell yourself the truth: you can't predict the future, you'll have bad days, and you aren't perfect. But you will be resilient after you read this book.

Now that you know some terminology and background, can see more clearly your own struggles with getting things done, and have a common language for talking about project management, let's drill down into each of the phases described in this book in more detail.

THE CHECKLIST (OVERVIEW)

The first letter of the words in the mnemonic given in Exhibit 1.1 will help you remember the four main phases of project management, which correspond to the main chapters of this book. The chapters are:

Define (Chapter 2)

Plan (Chapter 3)

Manage (Chapter 4)

Review (Chapter 5)

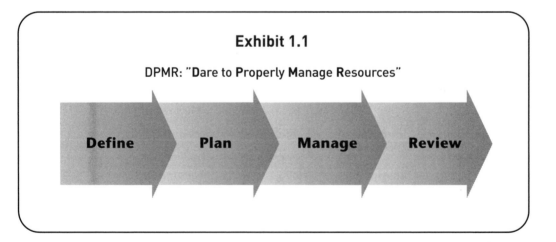

Exhibit 1.1

DPMR: "Dare to Properly Manage Resources"

Define → Plan → Manage → Review

Exhibit 1.2 shows a high-level flow for project management. Although this looks very orderly and linear, the lines between these phases are blurry. A real project proceeds through these steps more like a tornado—spinning, returning, and creating chaos. For example, even with best efforts during Define and Plan, something will surprise you when you get to Manage.

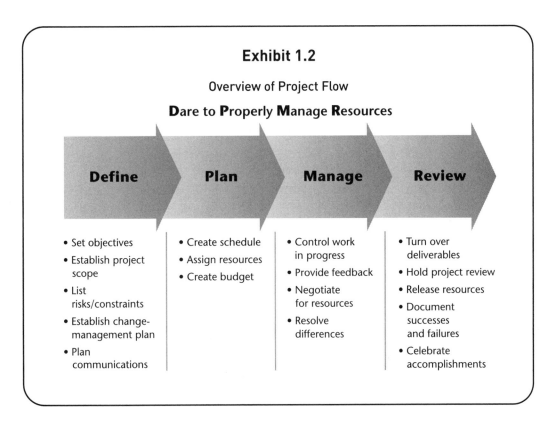

Exhibit 1.2

Overview of Project Flow

Dare to Properly Manage Resources

Define	Plan	Manage	Review
• Set objectives • Establish project scope • List risks/constraints • Establish change-management plan • Plan communications	• Create schedule • Assign resources • Create budget	• Control work in progress • Provide feedback • Negotiate for resources • Resolve differences	• Turn over deliverables • Hold project review • Release resources • Document successes and failures • Celebrate accomplishments

Remember, in the definition previously discussed, a project has a beginning and end. In between, four significant things occur:

Define* answers the question *why

Define explores *why* the project is being done. In other words, why is money being invested in this project instead of something else? The answers to this question begin to determine the business case, establishing the change this project is bringing to your organization. This is the most critical phase of this project is bringing to your organization. This is the most critical phase of project management and the one most often skipped in the pressure to get going. However, all the questions asked in this phase, as you'll see, have to be answered somewhere. If you don't take the time to discover the answers at the start of the project, the answers will be revealed as the project is in progress, and they will terrorize you. This is where the chapter quote, "Bad News early is Good News," becomes an important mantra to remember. As project managers, we are detectives, trying to uncover confusion or mistakes in understanding while it is easiest to react. We facilitate difficult discussions with others who would rather avoid them.

I call the deliverables of this phase the Project Charter. Other terms used to describe this phase, which you may hear others use, are Project Definition, Project Scope (which is a part of this phase), and Business Case.

Plan answers the question *how*

Plan determines *how* the project will be done to meet the business goals expressed in the earlier Define phase. An accurate plan cannot be built without understanding the questions answered in Define. Disastrous plans are often built when Define is skipped. The tasks to be done, the timing, the budget, and the people involved cannot be determined without understanding the context of the project established in Define. Even with a good project charter, it is very common in Plan to uncover new requirements that may change some of the things you thought to be true in Define, so you often jump back and forth between the two phases.

One of the reasons people think jumping straight into the project plan is acceptable may be connected to project management software such as Microsoft Project. This program does not really have functionality for Define. The strength of software tools is found in their ability to build and monitor a project plan. Many novice project managers assume that if it's okay for Microsoft Project to start at the project plan, that's where they should start too.

Other terms you may see to describe this phase of a project are Project Schedule, Critical Path, and Gantt chart. The last two of these tools—Critical Path and Gantt—are really tools that you may choose to create during this phase.

Manage requires seeking to *adapt*

Manage is the part of the project when the project plan is implemented. This is the phase where you find out all the elements of the project you didn't know about or you thought about inaccurately. At one time in my career I used the word *control* instead of *adapt*, but I have come to the conclusion that control is impossible. In fact, when you approach a project with the mindset of control, the result, when projects get off track, is self-blame and more internal stress. Thinking you can control a project also prevents you from being flexible to change during the project.

Staying agile and resilient is the best thing you can do for a project. It is human nature to feel like you're wasting time if you aren't working on the project, but taking a little time to Define and Plan is as much real work as the doing part of the project.

As the project progresses, unexpected glitches will test the mettle of the project manager. The Manage phase tends to toss the project manager back into Define and Plan frequently, either to reinforce the scope, objectives, or schedule or to make changes to objectives and schedule when the scope must change.

The deliverable of this phase is a finished project. Other terms used to describe this phase that you may hear are Deploy, Implement, or Roll Out.

Review requires seeking to *learn*

Once the project outcomes are delivered, the project is not really over. The last phase of project management is to *Review* the project so that the next project goes even better. In this phase, you will *learn* how to actually end a project, which is amazingly difficult to do. If you think about it, the people who asked for the project in the first place like discovering new functionality, so they keep the project going. The trick is to ensure that you've learned all you can before moving on to something new.

Although it's also important to do small debriefs throughout the project to capture lessons learned, after the project is closed out it's important to facilitate a debrief to learn what went well and what could have been done more effectively, from as many people as possible. This phase is also often skipped to hurry on to the next project. This curses the project managers to make the same mistakes over and over again on subsequent projects.

PROJECT MANAGEMENT IS DIFFERENT FROM A DEVELOPMENT PROCESS

Before you learn about each of these phases in detail in the following chapters, let's look at something that often confuses people about project management: the difference between project management and a development process.

Project management is a process for planning, organizing, and managing a project to a successful completion. A development process or methodology is a checklist for the work required to get the project done; in other words, it provides a template of the tasks that need to be done if the project is to be successful. Here are a few examples:

- If you are a trainer developing a workshop, there are methodologies and best practices that you can follow—for example, the ADDIE model (Analyze, Design, Develop, Implement, and Evaluate). This learning development methodology helps you identify the tasks that will need to be done to develop the project, which you discover during Plan.

- If you are developing a new product, there are methodologies you can follow, again based on the best practices. Information technology (IT) developers use different methodologies for different types of technical solutions. Again, the methodology used defines the (most) tasks for the project.

No matter what type of project you are doing, someone else has probably done something similar. In almost every industry, there are documented best practices that can help you determine what tasks need to be done. A quick search on the web will identify the best approach for you. In general, all of these methodologies break down into the following phases:

Analyze	Gather the requirements to solve the problem at hand
Design	Create a blueprint or strategy for solving the problem
Develop	Implement your strategy and build your solution
Implement	Transition to and deploy your new solution

Exhibit 1.3 shows you these phases and how they would relate to building a new house.

Exhibit 1.3

Building a House

Analyze	Determine the requirements	What kind of house do you want? How many rooms? Where will it be located?
Design	Create a blueprint	Architect will show you a couple of designs. You choose one based on what you've asked for.
Develop	Build	Construct the house.
Implement	Deploy	Move in.

Finally, we need to clarify one more phase after Implement that in truth isn't a phase at all, it's a process: Maintenance. Maintenance occurs after a project is complete. To transition to Maintenance is sometimes tricky and unclear. To avoid the frightening possibility that your project will never end (that is, never go to Maintenance), make sure that the completion criteria are established and agreed to early on.

You'll learn more about this in Chapter 5 ("Review"). In addition, Chapter 2 ("Define") shows you how to clarify the scope of your project, which will ensure that maintenance is not included in the scope. Mixing up maintenance and project work is easy to do, so it is very easy to accidentally expand the scope of the project without adding more time or resources.

As projects have grown in complexity over the last ten years, software has evolved that approaches project development in a different way. Rather than structure the entire project in one long path through analysis, design, development, and implementation, project teams have begun to ask their customers to prioritize small but functional parts of a project. These small project bits are built quickly using fast, dedicated teams composed of both subject-matter experts and developers. Project management is just as important for these new *agile* approaches used by organizations. The quicker, simple techniques in this book are useful for carrying out this small-piece project approach.

THE ROLES OF PROJECT MANAGEMENT

Project Manager

A *project manager*'s primary responsibility is to plan, organize, and manage a project. In a way, the project manager stands concurrently in three time zones: looking ahead to what is coming up, dealing with today's crisis, and looking back to learn from past tasks and experiences. As a project manager you need to create a project charter and a project plan. You must organize the roles and resources required to do the project and deal with how to adapt the project when all your plans change.

In rare cases you may have a project on your list that you are funding and sponsoring yourself. If you are both the project manager and the project sponsor (see next section), rethink the importance of the project. If there is no one else in the business really backing the project, it might not be a good investment of your time.

While the project manager's role is important, the most important role in the whole enterprise is that of the project sponsor.

Project Sponsor

The *project sponsor* is the person representing the needs of the organization. The project sponsor is usually the person who has requested the work and defines the business case for the investment. Most often the project sponsor is a senior leader in your organization. The project sponsor is so critical that if you do not know who it is, you should stop the project. If you do have a sponsor, it's unlikely that this role will remain a secret for long.

The project sponsor owns the project. It is their project backed by their request and their money. As project manager, you will manage this project for them, but it is not your project. This is a critical point. Many project managers lose their way because they think of the project as belonging to them. They make choices that should be made by the sponsor. They avoid communication with the sponsor to save time and make business decisions instead of asking the sponsor. The project struggles if this occurs. The analogy that I use is that of a nanny. While you are at work, a nanny takes care of your children, keeping them fed, safe, and happy. But you'd never expect a nanny to make education decisions for your children.

Having multiple project managers or project sponsors increases the risk of failure for a project. Without clear governance, projects wallow in meetings, changed agendas, and inertia. If at all possible, encourage your organizations to choose a single project manager and a single sponsor. It's okay to have steering committees, but choose a single person from the committee to play the project sponsor role.

Most project sponsors don't really know what it means to be a sponsor, and the project manager must help them understand the responsibilities and the criticality of that role. Exhibit 1.4 shows a great checklist developed by Joan Knutson, PMP (www.joanknutson.com), a leader in project management, especially in IT organizations. This checklist is a good tool to help a project manager set clear expectations with the project sponsor. The project sponsor is involved throughout the project making large scope, budget, and time decisions with the input, advice, and recommendations of the project manager.

Exhibit 1.4

Project Sponsor Checklist

The sponsor's most important job during the project is to ensure that the project objectives are clear and that the cost-benefit analysis makes the project a good investment of the company's resources.

Before the project begins:

- Why is this project needed? What's the problem being solved or the opportunity to be seized? How does it support our corporate goals?
- What are the objectives? What will the end result look like?
- What are the benefits? How will life be better when the project is over?
- How will we measure success? What is our baseline? What is our target?
- What areas of the organization will be affected? In what ways?

(continued)

(continued)

- Who needs to be involved? And how?
- What are the boundaries or scope of the project?
- What are the constraints—in time, in money, in quality?
- What can realistically be achieved within those constraints?
- Roughly how much will it cost and how long will it take?
- What are the risks? Can they be managed?
- Should we proceed?

  During the life of the project:

- Are we accomplishing what we planned to accomplish? Within the planned time frame? With the planned resources? Within budget?
- Is there anything I can do to facilitate your work?
- Are you getting the cooperation you need from the business units?
- Can we still achieve the objectives? Are they still of value to the organization?
- What are our alternatives? What are the pros and cons?
- Should the project be stopped?

  At project completion:

- Did we accomplish what we planned to accomplish? Within the planned time frame? With the planned resources? Within budget?
- How did we perform, based on our success criteria?
- Are plans in place to measure the predicted benefits?
- What lessons did we learn?
- What remains to be done?

Used with permission of www.joanknutson.com

Stakeholders

Stakeholders are the other key individuals who have a vested interest in your project. They are the people who contribute information or time to your project, or receive some deliverable from the project. The project sponsor is a special case of a stakeholder. It is important to be clear who the stakeholders are. In Chapter 2 ("Define") you will learn how identifying the stakeholders helps you define the scope of your project.

Sometimes your stakeholders forget that they are not the only ones getting something from the project. If this happens, then having a strong project sponsor really helps. The risk of project failure increases with each additional stakeholder because of the conflicts that occur between them. In Chapter 4 ("Manage") you will learn how to negotiate and manage the conflict that naturally occurs between stakeholders during a project.

Project Team

The *project team* is a group of dedicated individuals who are responsible for completing the project. They may be computer programmers, business analysts, training developers, or some other skilled practitioner. As I noted earlier, the days are long gone when project teams were composed of a project manager and project team members who worked full time on this single project. In today's work environment a dedicated project team is increasingly rare. Most people are working on multiple projects while concurrently managing other projects. This matrix approach to project work means that you may not have a project team or at least not one that is dedicated to the project. It might make more sense to think of these people as stakeholders, because they are temporary and only partially engaged. More on this in Chapter 2 ("Define").

Partnerships

The only way to project success is through *partnership*. The only way to partnership is to have information flowing from and to the project. The only way to flow information adequately is to communicate early and often. All the techniques that you will learn in this book are designed to help you give and receive the information needed quickly to create project success. You will learn to look for new information all the time. The earlier you find out bad news, the more time you have to adapt, using the techniques in this book.

SUMMARY CHECKLIST

- Project management became an official practice in 1969 with the beginning of the Project Management Institute in the United States, known as PMI (www.pmi.org).

- Confusing the projects, processes, and tasks on your to-do list increases frustration at work.

- "Dare to Properly Manage Resources" through the four phases of project management: Define (answers the question *why*), Plan (answers the question *how*), Manage (requires seeking to *adapt*), and Review (requires seeking to *learn*).

- Project management is a process for planning, organizing, and managing a project to a successful completion. A development process is a checklist for the work required to get the project done.

- A project manager's primary responsibility is to plan, organize, and manage a project.

- The project sponsor represents the needs of the organization and often pays for the project.

- Having multiple project managers or project sponsors dramatically increases the risk of failure for a project.

- Stakeholders are people who have a vested interest in your project and define the scope of your project.

- The only way to project success is through partnership. The only way to partnership is to have information flowing both ways. The only way to flow information adequately is to communicate early and often.

CHAPTER 2

Define

"Insanity is just a project constraint."

In this chapter, you will:

- Create a project charter (definition) in 45 minutes
- Establish the business goals
- Define the roles of a project: project manager, sponsor, stakeholders, team
- Create a visual scope diagram
- Write project objectives
- Determine the risks and do risk mitigation
- Establish the starting constraints
- Create a communications plan
- Create a governance plan (change management)
- Establish the partnerships required for successful projects
- Learn that project management is not too hard and academic for you to use every day

In Chapter 1, you learned to identify a project by a few simple criteria. These included:

- A project has a beginning and an end
- A project has an end that is clearly measurable when done correctly
- A project requires temporary resources, including people who may not be thrilled to be helping you

If you don't have the critical awareness that you are indeed working on a project, three side effects will likely doom your success:

1. You won't understand why the business wants this project done in the first place, so you will be unable to make strong, strategic decisions about changes.

2. You'll be managing tasks, one at a time, by the seat of your pants and likely will miss a few (or more).

3. You won't be clear who else has a vested interest in your project; these unknowns will show up late in your project, wreaking havoc on your scope.

In Exhibit 2.1, you'll recognize the project management model introduced in Chapter 1. Remember, it consists of these four phases:

Define answers the question *why*

Plan answers the question *how*

Manage requires seeking to *adapt*

Review requires seeking to *learn*

This chapter will focus on *Define* ("Dare" from "Dare to Properly Manage Resources").

CREATING A PROJECT CHARTER (DEFINITION) IN 45 MINUTES

The Define phase contains steps with visual techniques for answering, from multiple angles, the question:

Why is the enterprise spending money on my project instead of something else?

Define explores *why* the project is being done. In other words, why are resources being invested in this project instead of something else? The answers to this question, which you will learn how to obtain from the techniques in this chapter, build the business case for doing the project.

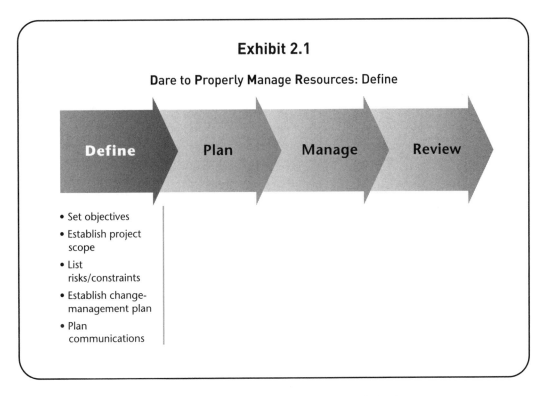

Exhibit 2.1

Dare to Properly Manage Resources: Define

Define → **Plan** → **Manage** → **Review**

- Set objectives
- Establish project scope
- List risks/constraints
- Establish change-management plan
- Plan communications

The Define phase establishes the change the project is bringing to your organization. By their nature, all projects bring change (or why would you do them?). Clearly, whenever change is coming, people get nervous and cautious. Having difficult conversations at the very beginning, when everyone is still playing nice and you have some political capital, is a smart move. Waiting to find out these critical answers until the project struggles, and everyone is angry, is a more difficult path—though a more typical one.

Define is the most critical phase of project management and the one most often skipped in the pressure to get going. In our heart of hearts, we all struggle to think of this as "real work." However, all the questions asked in this phase, as you'll see, have to be answered somewhere. If you don't take the time to discover the answers at the start of the project, the answers will be revealed, and will terrorize you, as the project is in progress.

The quote offered at the beginning of Chapter 1, "Bad News early is Good News," is an important mantra to remember. As project managers, we are detectives trying to uncover confusion or mistakes in understanding while it is easiest to react. Insanity will occur, as the line heading this chapter points out. It has nothing to do with our prowess as project managers; it's just a given.

I call the deliverables of the Define phase the Project Charter. Other terms used to describe this phase, which you may hear people use, include Project Definition, Project Scope (which is a part of this phase), and Business Case. Let's start with clarifying the business goals for the project.

ESTABLISHING THE BUSINESS GOALS

In Chapter 1, you read briefly about the project sponsor, who represents the business perspective and is accountable for the project meeting the needs of the business. Often, you will hear people talk about the return on investment (ROI) of a business investment. Projects should also provide an ROI for the investment required to get the project done. After all, why would you want to do a project that didn't add value to the business?

Imagine that the project sponsor was driving home from work and suddenly had an "aha" experience. Suppose the sponsor suddenly figures out a great solution to a difficult business challenge. To implement this solution will take many steps and resources, so by definition, this solution is a new project. The project sponsor already imagines a future with this new solution implementation complete and with the business gaining a distinct advantage over competitors. The sponsor of course doesn't know personally how to get all the tasks done, but knows exactly what the benefit to the business will be.

Figuring out the business objectives, or goals, is simply an attempt to quantify this "aha" experience. Remember that the sponsor is accountable for delivering this business value by sponsoring the project, as specified by the business objectives. Unfortunately, skipping doing and reviewing business objectives for a project tends to be a common mistake.

Business Case and Involvement

To figure out what the business objectives are, think about what I like to call the fictional Greek goddess of business: IRACIS. IRACIS stands for:

Increase Revenue

Avoid Cost

Improve Service

The value of every project can be described using these three very good reasons. In each project, one of these criteria trumps the others and is the *real* reason the project sponsor decided to allocate the resources to do the project.

In Exhibit 2.2, you can see the business objectives created for the "Day of Caring" project for Twillian Corporation. Notice that the IRACIS value "increase revenue," for example, is written out explicitly for each objective. (We will use this "Day of Caring" example throughout the book to think through other key project management principles.)

Exhibit 2.2

Business Objectives

Day of Caring
Project Sponsor: Ellen Whitney, VP of HR, Twillian Corp.
Project Manager: Sid Taylor, HR manager, Twillian Corp.
Business Objectives: The Day of Caring will provide the following value to Twillian Corp.:

1. Increase brand awareness in our marketplace, which will *increase our revenue*.

2. Improve service to our employees by encouraging them to participate in a positive project for the community. This will increase retention of employees, and *eliminate the cost* of rehiring.

3. *Improve service* to the community by providing free resources to complete projects.

It is also important that the business objectives be prioritized, as they are on this list. The project manager must know which is the most important business objective so that when the project plan is built, it reflects that reality. It may seem a bit harsh, but businesses, especially in tough times, have to ensure that the investments they make either make money or drive out cost. Service is nice, but only if it drives a cost or revenue goal as well.

Businesses often have to do projects to meet government regulations. What do you think the business objective would be for a project that will ensure compliance with new regulations? Sure, you have to do the project, but it's not going to increase your revenue; in fact, it may pull resources from the things that do increase revenue. Regulatory projects are always about avoiding cost—the cost of fines, lawsuits, and lawyers. This type of project needs to be done by a date, and as cheaply as possible, to avoid these costs.

Sometimes businesses do projects to gain a competitive advantage. For example, competing businesses might be leveraging social media, so yours has to also. There is no guarantee that this project will increase revenue, avoid cost, or improve service, but the business is hoping that it will at least bring in (or at least not lose) revenue. So it really all comes down to Increase Revenue and Avoid Cost.

Potential Challenges

At first glance, it seems that these business objectives are pretty straightforward and simple to create. Looking a little deeper, how would you measure that these business objectives were met? How much increased revenue can Twillian Corp. expect from participating in this volunteer project, and over what period of time? How will the company differentiate between increased revenue from other marketing efforts and this volunteer effort? And most important, will anyone really take the time to track this?

These are very difficult questions to answer. If you've ever tried to calculate the return on investment of a project, you know that it is often a mixture of real numbers and assumptions or magic. And it takes a lot of time, time most companies don't have right now. To approach an executive and ask for definitive, measurable answers to these questions on a project he or she has already decided to do is probably not career-enhancing. Instead, use these business objectives to get really clear about the sponsor's "aha" experience so that you can build the best project plan.

Notice how the following bad examples don't give you any information on what you are trying to accomplish from a business value perspective:

- This will make our employees happy
- It's the right thing to do for the community
- We've always done it this way

Who Should Be Involved?

Exhibit 2.3 shows what roles are involved in writing business objectives. Clearly, the project sponsor, who represents the business, has the final word on the business objectives. In the next section, you'll learn that it isn't always all that clear to sponsors themselves.

Exhibit 2.3

Business Objectives: Who Should Be Involved?

	PROJECT SPONSOR	PROJECT MANAGER
Achieve the business objectives.	ACCOUNTABLE	RESPONSIBLE
Create a draft of the business objectives.	CONSULTED	ACCOUNTABLE/ RESPONSIBLE
Approve and prioritize the draft of the business objectives.	RESPONSIBLE	ACCOUNTABLE
Ensure the business objectives are written and prioritized.	CONSULTED	ACCOUNTABLE/ RESPONSIBLE

ACCOUNTABLE: the buck stops here. RESPONSIBLE: does the task. CONSULTED: shares expertise.

Strategies for Influencing Stakeholders

It would be great if the project sponsor would write up the business objectives and give them to the project manager when starting a project. In reality, I have never heard of this happening. In most cases, the project sponsor is a busy executive and expects these things to be done by the project manager. The best strategy is for the project manager to draft up the business objectives and then ask the project sponsor to approve them and prioritize them, perhaps in a quick conversation.

It is not unusual for support groups to do projects that don't really have a project sponsor even though they have business objectives. For example, suppose the HR department decides to purchase software to track and manage the performance review process. It seems logical that the vice president of HR would be the sponsor for this project. However, the software is intended to be used for the entire company. The project will be much more effective if there is a sponsor from the business side, who may have an issue with the performance review process that the software will hopefully solve. When support groups create projects to help others but don't engage a sponsor from the area they are seeking to help, the projects struggle. This is also a critical step to begin the organizational change you'll learn more about in Chapter 4 ("Manage").

Using Sidebar 2.1, think about the business objectives for your project.

Sidebar 2.1

Writing Your Business Objectives

Try this for your project. Complete the phrase for each business objective by picking one of the reasons, explaining how that will occur, and then ranking them.

RANK	BUSINESS OBJECTIVE
	The project will [increase revenue, avoid cost, or improve service] by . . .
	The project will [increase revenue, avoid cost, or improve service] by . . .
	The project will [increase revenue, avoid cost, or improve service] by . . .
	The project will [increase revenue, avoid cost, or improve service] by . . .
	The project will [increase revenue, avoid cost, or improve service] by . . .

DETERMINING THE PROJECT SCOPE

Scope creep is the factor most mentioned as the thing that destroyed the success of the project. It is so common to start projects and have them morph into bigger projects. Project managers blame the stakeholders for changing their minds, and stakeholders blame the project managers for adding complexity that is really not necessary. Both are true.

Depending on your processing style, you may take one or two steps to start building scope diagrams. If you tend to be more analytical and detailed, you may start with a table like that found in Exhibit 2.4 for our Day of Caring example. If you are more visual and nonlinear as a thinker, you may skip this step and go straight to the diagram in Exhibit 2.5. In either case, it might be best to try both just to figure out what works for you.

Either way, you are working to discover two things:

1. "Who will provide necessary guidance to the project team while building the solution?" Some people call these the *inputs* to the project. This may include some or all of the following questions:

   - Who will provide the requirements—the specifications of what's needed?
   - Who will be writing the check for the work? Who manages the budget?
   - Who will tell you what processes or standards need to be followed?
   - Who will provide the technology needed?
   - Who will provide the people you will need (and determine if you will need or get more)?
   - Who will do the design work?
   - Who will do the testing or compliance work?

2. You will also ask yourself, "Who or what (for example, systems) will receive things from this project?" Some people call these the *output* of the project. This may include some or all of the following questions:

   - To whom will the project deliver reports?
   - Who will receive the final deliverables of the project?
   - What systems will the project have to build interfaces to?
   - Who will do the training for the rollout, and what do they need to do this?
   - Who will do marketing and sales for the roll-out, and what do they need to do this?

These answers are entered into the simple table in Exhibit 2.4. Take a look at this table now, and look at the first stakeholder listed, the project sponsor. To get the project done, the sponsor, over time, will *contribute*:

- Business objectives
- Budget
- Dates
- Resources
- Decisions

Exhibit 2.4

Scope Brainstorming Table

STAKEHOLDER	INPUT TO PROJECT	OUTPUT RECEIVED FROM PROJECT	COMMENTS
Project sponsor	Business objectives Budget Dates Resources Decisions	Status updates Major scope changes Recommended adjustments to the project plan	
Staff	Availability Desired volunteer activity Feedback	Schedule Feedback survey Request for volunteers	
Charity organization	Volunteer opportunities Location Hours United Way contact person	Volunteers Schedule Twillian contact person	
Catering	Proposal Contract Invoice Boxed lunches	Request for proposal Signed contract Payment	Not sure about payment—this will probably come directly from purchasing
Purchasing	Recommended caterer Request for proposal Signed contract	Information about box lunch (numbers, date, special needs)	
CEO	Request for participation Schedule Boxed lunch	Final volunteer hours report	
IT staff	Away notices	Date required	

The project sponsor will *receive* things as the project progresses as well, including:

- Status updates
- Major scope changes

This same reasoning is documented for each of the stakeholders involved in the project. Notice that this table helps you work out who the stakeholders are, what they provide to the project to get it done, and what they get from the project.

Use Sidebar 2.2 to build a table of stakeholders for your project.

Now we'll use the table to help us build our scope diagram. The scope diagram for the Day of Caring project is shown in Exhibit 2.5. Notice that

---

Sidebar 2.2

Table to Prepare for Your Scope Diagram

Using this table, brainstorm who the stakeholders are for your project. Then complete the inputs and outputs that will occur during the project. Finally, use the comment column to jot down "aha's" you have as you go through this brainstorming activity.

STAKEHOLDER	INPUT TO PROJECT	OUTPUT RECEIVED FROM PROJECT	COMMENTS
Project sponsor (Name:)	Business objectives Budget Dates Resources Decisions	Status updates Major scope changes Recommended adjustments to the project plan	

Exhibit 2.5

Scope Diagram

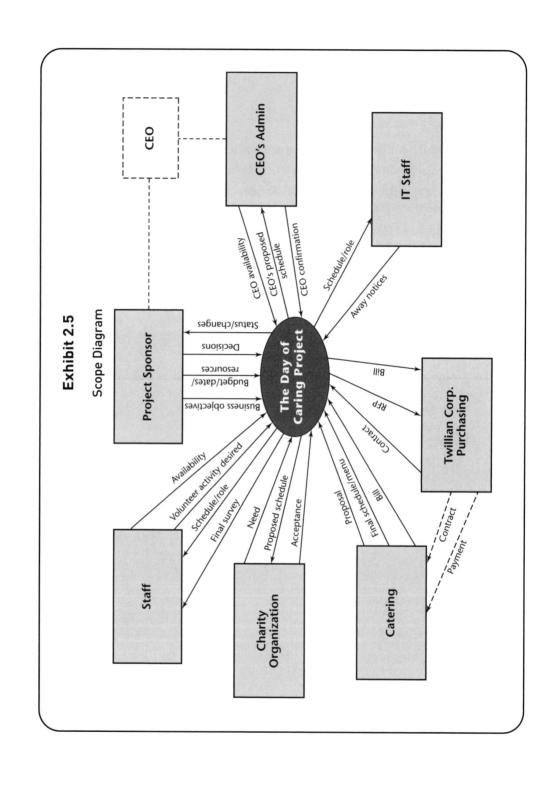

each of the stakeholders from the first column of the table is shown as a box positioned around the center, which represents the project. You are the project manager in the project, so you're not shown as a stakeholder. The arrows to the project from the stakeholders come directly from the input column, and the arrows going the other way come from the output column. It's important to note that the brainstorming table is not a substitute for the scope diagram; it is a technique to make the drawing of the scope diagram simpler. This table can certainly be saved with the other project documentation, but there is no need to keep it up-to-date.

Be aware that when you draw your scope diagram, you may discover that your table assumptions are not exactly correct, just like in this example. For instance, at Twillian it is required that you work through purchasing on any large contracts. Notice how the flow of arrows between purchasing, the caterer, and the project are different from the initial arrangements in the table.

You may also notice the dotted line. This indicates a conversation that is happening without the Project Manager. It is 'against the rules' to draw solid lines between stakeholders, which would indicate a flow of information that the Project Manager has in scope but doesn't know about, so it makes no sense. Instead, using dotted lines helps show significant conversations that are occurring that influence the project but are out of scope. Finally, the project manager won't work directly with the CEO. All discussions will go through the CEO's administrative person.

The Magic of a Scope Diagram

The scope diagram will be updated throughout the project and will reflect changes as the project progresses. It's perfectly fine to skip the table if you feel comfortable drawing the scope diagram directly.

To minimize confusion on the scope diagram while maintaining the true complexity of the project, some of the words are combined or aggregated to a broader term. For example, instead of putting an arrow from the project to the project sponsor for each of the bullets from the table (status updates, major scope changes, and recommended adjustments to the project plan), I've combined them into two arrows: decisions and status/changes.

Using Sidebar 2.3, convert the table you just created for your project into a scope diagram. In class, our students build these scope diagrams using Post-its

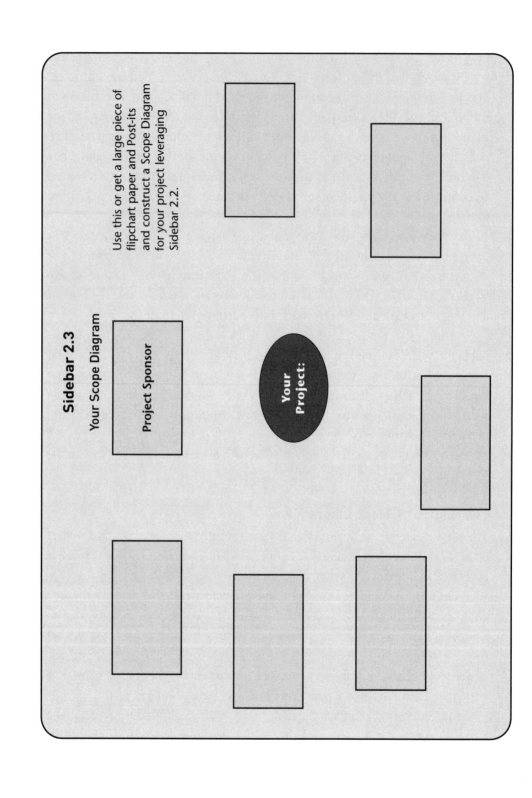

Sidebar 2.3

Your Scope Diagram

Use this or get a large piece of flipchart paper and Post-its and construct a Scope Diagram for your project leveraging Sidebar 2.2.

Project Sponsor

Your Project:

on a piece of flipchart paper, and then draw the arrows with pencil. If you use this technique, put one color of Post-it in the center to represent the project and use a different color for all the stakeholders. Remember to use dotted lines if you are tempted to add arrows between stakeholders.

The scope diagram explains more than reams of narrative description. It is the visual representation, the story, of your project. This easily created diagram—it can take less than 30 minutes—builds a base that creates the following advantages for a project.

Four Advantages of a Scope Diagram

1. A scope diagram creates a picture of the complexity of a project; the more stakeholders and arrows, the more difficult and risky the project. This complexity is communicated to stakeholders when this picture is reviewed, helping to solve the eternal problem of managing the unrealistic expectations of stakeholders at the start of a project. This is the antidote to "How hard can it be?"

2. A scope diagram creates a base to build a quick project communication strategy. Each of the stakeholders needs to receive communication. Each arrow shows what each stakeholder cares about. These can be put in a table easily along with a strategy for communication frequency and content. In Chapter 3 you will learn how to create a simple spreadsheet that is often enough communication for most stakeholders.

3. A scope diagram creates a base to brainstorm the project tasks from. The arrows show information flowing. For information to flow, work has to be done by someone. If the arrow is coming from the project, the work is done by the project team. If the arrow is coming from the stakeholder, this stakeholder is responsible for the work. Chapter 3 will also show you how to move from the scope diagram to the project schedule.

4. A scope diagram clarifies roles and makes it easier to see who is responsible for what. The most important clarification is that of the project sponsor. The governance, which is the decision-making process for change during the project, is another process that can be jump-started by understanding and communicating the scope diagram.

One of the side effects of using a scope diagram as a means of organization is that it becomes evident early on that not only are your projects pretty complex, but you are stakeholders on other people's projects you didn't even know about. This is a good thing—bad news early is good news—but it doesn't feel like good news. You may see that reaction from others as well.

Who Should Be Involved?

The table in Exhibit 2.6 reinforces the importance of clarifying up front with the project sponsor which efforts on the project will require their time and which will not. Notice that the project manager has the accountability and responsibility, and the project sponsor, consulted, has gone back to his or her other responsibilities after being responsible for approving the initial scope diagram. The table also shows how much the project manager drives the involvement of others. If stakeholders are not showing up at meetings, it's the project manager's responsibility to get them to the table or figure out a way to get the job done without them.

Exhibit 2.6

ARCI* Scope Table

	PROJECT SPONSOR	PROJECT MANAGER	STAKEHOLDERS
Create the scope diagram.	CONSULTED	ACCOUNTABLE/ RESPONSIBLE	CONSULTED
Share the business objectives and scope diagram with the stakeholders to clarify requirements and manage expectations.	CONSULTED	ACCOUNTABLE/ RESPONSIBLE	CONSULTED
Approve the initial scope diagram.	RESPONSIBLE	ACCOUNTABLE	INFORMED

*ARCI: ACCOUNTABLE: the buck stops here. RESPONSIBLE: does the task. CONSULTED: shares expertise. INFORMED: told about the task.

Notice that the stakeholders are shown as consulted on the initial draft of the scope diagram. Their input is critical and likely will change many things on the model. However, projects run by complete democracy are generally not successful. Scope creep can easily occur during this review process; it is the responsibility of the project manager to protect the scope specified by the business objectives and the project sponsor.

Here's another way to validate your scope diagram's completeness. Using the analogy of building a house, Exhibit 2.7 shows a basic four-phase approach to developing anything. You may notice that this is just a basic problem-solving process. When creating a scope diagram, thinking through basic steps like these can help you identify stakeholders and deliverables.

Exhibit 2.7

Phases of New Development

PHASE	DEFINITION	BUILDING A HOUSE
Analyze	Figure out what the problem is.	Determine the basic needs: how many bedrooms, bath, location, square footage, etc.
Design	Sketch out a detailed solution.	Create a blueprint of the house desired.
Build	Build the solution, adjusting to surprises.	Construct the house, adjusting to surprises.
Implement	Roll the solution out.	Move in to the house.

Now pretend you are creating a new workshop that your company is going to sell to its customers. Different people would be involved as stakeholders in each phase (Analyze, Design, Build, and Implement). This is a good time to think of any stakeholders that you might have missed.

Finally, remember in the beginning of Chapter 1 when we discussed the difference between a project and a process? That is a critical difference when you draw a scope diagram. Don't include the *maintenance* of whatever you are building when the project is complete. Maintenance is a process and generally has no end point.

Potential Challenges

One of the most common issues that can come up while doing a scope diagram is confusion about the sponsor. Sometimes you can't figure out who the sponsor is, and sometimes there simply isn't one. Your best bet is to very publicly delay the project until a sponsor comes forward. Moving the project forward without a sponsor usually doesn't end well.

For example, suppose you have found a new software application that would simplify prioritization of incoming email. It sounds almost too good to be true, and it would be surprising if every employee didn't need the software. As you scope out the project, you find out that *you* are the sponsor, and that no one has really asked for this software. Implementation will be difficult and success unlikely unless you find someone who thinks there is a business need for this solution. Even the best software rollouts bomb without developing a business need, which is the role of the project sponsor.

Equally detrimental to the project is when you have multiple project sponsors. This situation isn't that unusual, especially when the project crosses multiple departments within an organization. For example, suppose you are rolling out a new process and software that will streamline the current performance review process. Every supervisor and employee will be impacted by this change, so it makes sense that the project sponsorship be shared between department vice presidents to ensure equal commitment. This is common and logical, but it's deadly to project success. When there is more than one voice voting on every scope, budget, requirement, or schedule question, the project will barely move forward. In these situations, you should encourage the formation of a committee with a spokesperson who will be your project sponsor and who will also keep the rest of the committee in the loop.

In some special situations, a stakeholder is actually a system. For example, if you are a trainer rolling out a new online workshop that will be run through a web-based LMS (learning management system), you might draw an arrow on a visual project plan from the project to the LMS that shows the final course upload. However, you are more likely to contact a person working in the LMS area to upload, so even in this situation an actual person is really your stakeholder.

Strategies for Influencing Stakeholders

A natural part of the project process is the work of creating consensus between stakeholders about what is inside and outside the scope of the project. If you are the project manager, negotiating this conversation is your job.

When stakeholders request more work at this point in the project, it may be possible to include it. However, when scope increases are requested during the project—which will happen—the project manager's first response is usually *No*. This should be your last line of defense, not your first response. Instead, consider language like this: "Yes, we can consider including your option, but the impact on the entire project will be . . . " Here is an example:

> **Stakeholder:** The board of directors must approve every communication created for the Day of Caring.
>
> **Project Manager:** Yes, that's possible, and the impact will be that since the board only meets once a month, it will be impossible to hit the date we have published. Another option is for the board to choose a representative who will do this review more quickly. What are your thoughts on how to get this done?

If the stakeholder stays persistent and maybe gets irrational, it is necessary for a project manager to get the project sponsor involved. In such difficult times, a project sponsor is an invaluable tiebreaker. Still, your project sponsor wants you to handle everything you possibly can on your own, so this technique should be used sparingly.

Stakeholders want project managers to lead. It is critical for the project manager to manifest leadership behavior early to set the culture and expectations for the increasingly difficult conversations that will occur as the project progresses.

DETERMINING THE PROJECT OBJECTIVES

Project objectives are the contract the project manager makes with the business. After completing the business objectives and scope diagram and reviewing these with the sponsor and stakeholders, you will have the knowledge to create the initial sketch of the project objectives.

The project objectives are the metrics for project success. The business objectives are the metrics for the return on the project investment that came from the deliverables of the project. In contrast, the project objectives are how to measure the quality of the deliverables.

Project objectives determine how the success of the project will be measured:

- *What* will the outcomes be?
- *How* will they be measured?
- *Who* will measure them?

Who Should Be Involved?

The project objectives are creating a clear metric for successful completion of the project. It's very likely, though, that people will resist talking about it specifically enough. Use Exhibit 2.8 to identify whom you will work with and what their role will be during the finalization of this critical document.

Exhibit 2.8

ARCI* Project Objectives

	PROJECT SPONSOR	PROJECT MANAGER	STAKEHOLDERS
Identify the project objectives.	CONSULTED	ACCOUNTABLE/ RESPONSIBLE	CONSULTED
Share the project objectives and scope diagram with the stakeholders to clarify requirements and manage expectations.	CONSULTED	ACCOUNTABLE/ RESPONSIBLE	CONSULTED
Approve the project objectives.	RESPONSIBLE	ACCOUNTABLE	INFORMED

*ARCI: ACCOUNTABLE: the buck stops here. RESPONSIBLE: does the task. CONSULTED: shares expertise. INFORMED: told about the task.

Technique: Writing Project Objectives

Exhibit 2.9 shows different categories of project objectives.

Exhibit 2.9

Project Objectives

How will the success of this project be measured?
What will the outcomes be?
How will they be measured?
Who will measure them?

Learning Objectives:
- Measurable change in behavior/bridge the gap
- **A**udience, **B**ehavior, **C**ondition, **D**egree
- What can they do NOW that they couldn't do THEN?

The volunteers will learn to collaborate with others to achieve a common goal.

System Objectives (E-learning)
- SLAs (Service Level Agreement): Availability of system ("up time")
- Backups
- Security
- Maintainability of Software/Standard Objects
- Response Time

The volunteer schedule will be available 24/7 through SharePoint.

Project Goals:
- Budget/Schedule
- Government Regulation
- Resources Used
- Media (maybe)

Three media outlets will be present at the Day of Caring.

© Russell Martin and Associates; www.russellmartin.com

If you are creating a learning experience (workshop, online training, job aid, and so on), you will create learning objectives as part of your list of project objectives. Learning objectives determine what the learners will be able to do after the experience that they can't do now. For more information about writing good learning objectives, check out my book *Project Management for Trainers*.

There are up to four parts of a learning objective, with the last two dependent on the skill gap:

A. Audience: who will be learning? (required)

Determining the existing skill sets, demographics, and business and educational background will help clarify the gap between today's behavior and what is desired in the future. The tighter and clearer the audience, the more likely the learning will occur. Put another way, the broader the audience, the more difficult it is to clarify the gap and build relevant learning materials.

B. Behavior: what behavior will change? (required)

This specifies the behavior you are hoping to change as the learning progresses. Generally, this specifies a skill or knowledge change. Avoid using any behaviors you won't be able to measure in class, for example, "understanding" or "know." Replace these with words like "define," "list," and "contrast."

C. Condition: under what condition will this learning occur? (optional)

Sometimes your learners will be able to leverage user guides or job aids to remember how to do things. Many times in your workshop you may end up teaching them how to find the answer rather than memorize the answer. Learning to use complex software applications usually is best approached by showing learners how to find the answers themselves, since with new releases these constantly change. The condition might be "Using the online Help function," for example.

D. Degree: what is the level of perfection required in doing this new behavior? (optional)

In some situations, for example safety training, learners must be able to prove that they are 100 percent competent. Never put a number for the degree of competency unless you intend to measure it with practice activities and a pre- and post-test.

Exhibit 2.10 shows an example of a learning objective for the Day of Caring project.

Using the scope diagram and business objectives that you have created, use Sidebar 2.4 to create the project objectives for your project.

Exhibit 2.10

Learning Objective: Day of Caring Project

Volunteer day will be a success when:

- 30%–50% of all employees are involved
- Projects have a minimum duration of two hours and a maximum duration of five hours (9AM–2PM)
- At least one on-site assembly project is included for employees who cannot leave the worksite

Sidebar 2.4

Your Project Objectives

> How will the success of this project be measured?
>
> *What* will the outcomes be?
>
> *How* will they be measured?
>
> *Who* will measure them?

Learning Objectives:
- Measurable change in behavior/bridge the gap
- **A**udience, **B**ehavior, **C**ondition, **D**egree
- What can they do NOW that they couldn't do THEN?

1.
2.
3.

System Objectives

SLAs (Service Level Agreement): Availability of system ("up time")

- Backups
- Security
- Maintainability of Software/Standard Objects
- Response Time

1.
2.
3.

Project Goals:
- Budget/Schedule
- Government Regulation
- Resources Used
- Media (maybe)

1.
2.
3.

DETERMINING RISK AND MITIGATION

Admittedly, thinking about risk this early in the process is pretty depressing. It doesn't seem a necessary step now when it's more fun to bask in the possibilities of a perfect project. Remember, bad news early is good news; once again, the techniques help discover the bad things early enough to react and save the project. These discussions are not easy or fun, but they are very helpful as your project moves along.

Risk, by definition, is the *likelihood* of something happening to threaten the success of a project. Success is determined by three things—time, cost, and quality—so risk is the chance of something threatening any or all of these. A given threat may never arise, or one may occur that you never saw coming. The purpose of these techniques is to assess risk, so that you will see threats faster and know what to do more quickly.

Who Should Be Involved?

The three steps of risk mitigation are detailed in Exhibit 2.11. Notice the slight difference from scope and project objectives. The involvement of stakeholders and even the sponsor is determined by you and driven by the politics of the project. Sometimes it is not a good idea to start talking about horrible things that might happen. Your decision to refrain from this disclosure might be because of the personality of the stakeholders or because of the culture of your organization. Still, the more people you get to help brainstorm these risks, the better. This is especially true if the stakeholders are doing work or are experts in areas that you know little about.

Technique: Quick and Dirty Risk Assessment

Exhibit 2.12 shows the criteria for doing the Quick and Dirty Risk Assessment. There are three important criteria:

Size	How big is the project relative to others that the team has done?
Structure	How stable are the requirements?
Technology	Will there be new technology and/or processes used to do the project?

Exhibit 2.11

ARCI* Risk Mitigation

	PROJECT SPONSOR	PROJECT MANAGER	STAKEHOLDERS
Determine the Quick and Dirty Risk Assessment number.	INFORMED/ CONSULTED	ACCOUNTABLE/ RESPONSIBLE	INFORMED/ CONSULTED
Determine the risks possible for the project, their likelihood, impact on the project, and mitigation.	INFORMED/ CONSULTED	ACCOUNTABLE/ RESPONSIBLE	INFORMED/ CONSULTED
Share the risk mitigation strategy with appropriate stakeholders.	INFORMED/ CONSULTED	ACCOUNTABLE/ RESPONSIBLE	INFORMED/ CONSULTED

*ARCI: ACCOUNTABLE: the buck stops here. RESPONSIBLE: does the task. CONSULTED: shares expertise. INFORMED: told about the task.

Exhibit 2.12

Quick and Dirty Risk Assessment: Day of Caring Project

RISK COMPONENT	ASSESSMENT (1 = SMALLEST RISK; 10 = LARGEST RISK)	DAY OF CARING PROJECT
Size (how big is this project compared to others your team has done?)	1 (small compared to others we've done) to 10 (largest project we've ever done)	2
Structure (how stable are the requirements relative to other projects your team has done?)	1 (the requirements are set) to 10 (there are no requirements)	3
Technology (how big a learning curve will there be for your team on the technology and/or processes you'll use on this project?)	1 (no new technology or process) to 10 (brand-new technology and process)	3
AVERAGE (Sum all three and divide by 3)		2.6

The risk for each criterion is assessed from 1 to 10. The higher the number, the more risk for the project. The third column shows the Quick and Dirty Risk Assessment for the Day of Caring project. Look in the second column for an explanation as to why the number was picked.

Your best-guess assessment numbers for size, structure, and technology are averaged, as you can see in the exhibit. The final number is the risk of the project failing: 2.6 means that there's a 2.6 out of 10 chance the project will fail. At first, this seems like a pretty bold prediction based on a small amount of data, but you are evaluating the three most common factors that create failure, and you are judging your evaluation based on your intuition and the experience of your team. Project management research has shown that the best estimates come from historical experience, and the best risk prediction comes from your expert intuition. You work there, you know the people and culture—you know.

Sidebar 2.5 provides you with a worksheet to complete the Quick and Dirty Risk Assessment for one of your projects. Remember to pick a number that is relative to your experience and the expertise of the stakeholders you will work with on the project.

Sidebar 2.5

Your Quick and Dirty Risk Assessment

RISK COMPONENT	ASSESSMENT (1 = SMALLEST RISK; 10 = LARGEST RISK)	YOUR PROJECT
Size (how big is this project compared to others your team has done?)	1 (small compared to others we've done) to 10 (largest project we've ever done)	
Structure (how stable are the requirements relative to other projects your team has done?)	1 (the requirements are set) to 10 (there are no requirements)	
Technology (how big a learning curve will there be for your team on the technology and/or processes you'll use on this project?)	1 (no new technology or process) to 10 (brand-new technology and process)	
AVERAGE (Sum all three and divide by 3)		

Decision Guidelines

Exhibit 2.13 offers a guideline for deciding what to do using the numbers your risk analysis generated. Notice that the higher the number, the more time you should spend thinking about what types of risk may occur and what you can do about it. Lower numbers indicate that you don't need to complete a more detailed analysis. In other words, sketch out a quick plan (Chapter 3) and just do it.

Exhibit 2.13

Quick and Dirty Risk Mitigation: Decision Guidelines

RISK: AVERAGE ASSESSMENT NUMBER	HOW TO PROCEED
1–4	No need to do anything else. Your higher-risk projects probably will require more of your time. Move on to Chapter 3 and build a quick schedule, then follow it.
5–8	Proceed to the next technique: do a risk mitigation table and determine how to avoid the higher risks if possible, or how to react if problems do occur, if that's all you can do.
9–10	You are in trouble. This project is going to take *more* than all your time, so try to clear your calendar as much as possible. The likelihood of project failure is high, so in addition to doing the risk mitigation table, start talking with the project sponsor and stakeholders on ways you might narrow the scope if (when?) things go bad.

As the table indicates, if the risk assessment number is 5 or greater, it's a good idea to do the next technique (risk mitigation table). If the risk is a 9 or 10, you've got a scary project and it might be a good time to think about how you will narrow the scope and reduce the risk of this project.

Use Sidebar 2.6 to create your own strategy.

Sidebar 2.6

Your Quick and Dirty Risk Mitigation: Next Steps

RISK AVERAGE NUMBER	HOW TO PROCEED	YOUR PROJECT STRATEGY
1–4	No need to do anything else. Your higher-risk projects probably will require more of your time. Move on to Chapter 3 and build a quick schedule, then follow it.	
5–8	Proceed to the next technique: do a risk mitigation table and determine how to avoid the higher risks if possible, or how to react if problems do occur, if that's all you can do.	
9–10	You are in trouble. This project is going to take *more* than all your time, so try to clear your calendar as much as possible. The likelihood of project failure is high, so in addition to doing the risk mitigation table, start talking with the project sponsor and stakeholders on ways you might narrow the scope if (when?) things go bad.	

Technique: Risk Mitigation Table

First, remember that you won't be using this technique unless your Quick and Dirty risk is 5 or greater. This is not meant to be a lengthy exercise: limit your time to an hour or less and do it with other stakeholders if possible. If this collaboration is not possible, then you'll still find great value by doing this table on your own.

Exhibit 2.14 shows a risk mitigation table. The first column shows the risks that you think might occur. The second shows what you think the likelihood of this risk is (high, medium, or low), and the next shows what you think the impact would be on the project (high, medium, low). Given this risk factor, you then think about whether there is anything you can do proactively to prevent the risk from occurring, and anything you can do reactively if the risk does occur. Exhibit 2.14 shows the risk mitigation table for the Day of Caring project.

Exhibit 2.14

Risk Mitigation Table: Day of Caring Project

POSSIBLE RISK	LIKELIHOOD	IMPACT ON PROJECT	PROACTIVE	REACTIVE
Charity is not participating this year.	M	M	Contact charity immediately.	Work with United Way to find alternative charities.
Volunteers are not available.	L	L	Communicate specific hours, need, dates as early as possible.	Ask people to bring a friend; get support from upper management.
Web space is time-consuming and unstable.	H	M	Commit time to learning capacity before rollout.	Stop using it; replace with Google Docs.

H: high M: medium L: low

Use Sidebar 2.7 to create a risk mitigation table for your own project. Chances are that one or two of the numbers from your Quick and Dirty Risk Assessment are higher than the others. This is the first place you should focus on to brainstorm mitigating risks that might occur. As you do this, you'll notice that your instincts take over. Sometimes there are no proactive things you can do. However, you do have one great reactive possibility: stop the project.

Sidebar 2.7

Your Risk Mitigation Table

POSSIBLE RISK	LIKELIHOOD (H, M, L)	IMPACT ON PROJECT (H, M, L)	PROACTIVE	REACTIVE

H: high M: medium L: low

Be brutally honest with yourself as you think through risk mitigation and pay attention to any danger points that caused you to worry during early discussion about the project. If your risk is 8–10, focus on size, structure, and technology as you complete this technique.

Potential Challenges

I have found on my own projects that *likelihood* can have a dark side. For example, if I decide that something is low likelihood, I pretend as if there is no chance of something going wrong this way in the project. I become blind to the risk as a possibility. Some of the most devastating impacts to some of my projects resulted from risks I thought were highly unlikely. Although using this column is consistent with best practices of project management, I don't include this column in my project management process. You may find it useful, so experiment with it to see if it's useful in your project planning.

Strategies for Influencing Stakeholders

No one wants to hear bad news at the start of a project, so the topic is often avoided. However, this is a critical tool for managing stakeholder expectations and sponsor expectations. Go over your risk mitigation table with the sponsor and important stakeholders and get their feedback. To keep things less emotional, remind stakeholders that risks are things that *may* or *may not* occur during the project.

ESTABLISHING THE STARTING CONSTRAINTS

Constraints create a lot of stress and challenge for the project manager and stakeholders, but that does not change the reality of their potential impact. It's important to accept the reality and create a strategy and project plan that work within those constraints.

Using this technique requires prioritizing the three main levers of project management—time, cost, and quality. Think of quality as a two-sided coin. One side is quality and the other is scope (more on this in Exhibit 2.16).

Who Should Be Involved?

Exhibit 2.15 helps determine who should be involved during discussions about constraints and the prioritization of project constraints.

Exhibit 2.15

ARCI* Constraints

	PROJECT SPONSOR	PROJECT MANAGER	STAKEHOLDERS
Determine the prioritization of the constraints.	INFORMED/ CONSULTED	ACCOUNTABLE/ RESPONSIBLE	INFORMED/ CONSULTED
Share constraints strategy with appropriate stakeholders.	INFORMED/ CONSULTED	ACCOUNTABLE/ RESPONSIBLE	INFORMED/ CONSULTED

*ARCI: ACCOUNTABLE: the buck stops here. RESPONSIBLE: does the task. CONSULTED: shares expertise. INFORMED: told about the task.

Technique: Determining Constraints

Exhibit 2.16 shows the constraints for the Day of Caring project. Notice that the constraints are listed on the left side, and that quality and scope are in the same cell. Across the top we have only three choices: can't get more, can't get much more, and will negotiate. For the Twillian Day of Caring the date is set, so it cannot be moved. You have more to do as a result. The budget may have a little leeway, but there certainly is not an unlimited budget for this philanthropic effort. That means that you will have to negotiate either quality or scope.

Exhibit 2.16

Constraints: Day of Caring Project

CONSTRAINT	CAN'T HAVE ANY MORE	CAN'T HAVE MUCH MORE	NEGOTIATE THIS
Time	X		
Cost		X	
Quality/Scope			X

You might explain the concept to your sponsor and stakeholders by pointing out that if you are out of time and out of money there are only two choices: one, do a smaller, critical piece of the project at the quality required; or two, do the whole project with very poor quality (I like to say "crappy" here). Often we delude ourselves by confusing hours of heroics (how hard we've worked) with high-quality project deliverables. Tell yourself the truth. The email you send at 1:30AM is usually not a good strategy.

As the comedian Stephen Wright once said, "You can't have everything. Where would you put it?" A project plan will be entirely different for a cost-constrained project than it is for a time-driven or quality-focused project. Use Sidebar 2.8 to figure out what the priorities are for one of your own projects. When you're done, check with your project sponsor and key stakeholders to see if they agree.

Potential Challenges

Some project managers list their priorities across the top (no. 1 priority through no. 3 priority), but I believe this confuses everyone. Who wants to address quality as the last priority? It hinders the conversation. Besides, there is a natural tension between time, cost, and quality.

Sidebar 2.8

Your Constraints

Put *one checkmark only* in each column and each row to show what you can negotiate on your project and what you cannot.

CONSTRAINT	CAN'T HAVE ANY MORE	CAN'T HAVE MUCH MORE	NEGOTIATE THIS
Time			
Cost			
Quality/Scope			

Strategies for Influencing Stakeholders

This technique sets the baseline for how you will negotiate with your project sponsor and stakeholders during the Manage phase of the project (Chapter 4). You can have this difficult conversation now or deal with the hysterics of the conversation that may occur later. The choice is yours.

CREATING A COMMUNICATIONS STRATEGY

As mentioned earlier, the project scope diagram provides a great way to jump-start the communication plan since it details how you are going to communicate with the stakeholders of your project. In Chapter 3, you will learn how to build a quick table to communicate with all your stakeholders. In some projects, especially with higher risk, it is politically prudent to communicate differently with various stakeholders. This technique can be used to set up a strategy for doing just that.

Who Should Be Involved?

Exhibit 2.17 shows the people you should involve during the discussion and prioritization of constraints.

Exhibit 2.17

ARCI* Communications Plan

	PROJECT SPONSOR	PROJECT MANAGER	STAKEHOLDERS
Determine the communication plan for each stakeholder.	INFORMED/ CONSULTED	ACCOUNTABLE/ RESPONSIBLE	INFORMED/ CONSULTED
Share the communication plan with appropriate stakeholders.	INFORMED/ CONSULTED	ACCOUNTABLE/ RESPONSIBLE	INFORMED/ CONSULTED

*ARCI: ACCOUNTABLE: the buck stops here. RESPONSIBLE: does the task. CONSULTED: shares expertise. INFORMED: told about the task.

Technique: Communications Plan

In Exhibit 2.18, you see that the Twillian Day of Caring project will require communications to be slightly different for the project sponsor, volunteers, and catering than it will for all the other stakeholders. Notice that there is no direct communication with the CEO (who is not a stakeholder, if you look back at the scope diagram), but the communication with the project sponsor provides a way for the sponsor to communicate with the CEO.

Use Sidebar 2.9 to create a communications plan for your project if differentiation for different stakeholders is necessary. Notice that the two columns in the middle show how the communication will differ in terms of frequency (how often you will communicate) and medium (what form the communication will take). Email is by far the most common way of communicating, but may be inappropriate politically. All communication will become a task on your project schedule (Chapter 3).

Potential Challenges

The biggest danger in communication is to not do it. No news is *bad* news. If your stakeholders do not hear from you, they will assume you are in trouble. It is better to proactively manage expectations.

Exhibit 2.18

Communications Plan: Day of Caring Project

STAKEHOLDER	FREQUENCY	MEDIUM	COMMENTS
CEO	Twice a month	One-page document emailed from my boss	Graph, calendar, status
Catering	Monthly	Summary of logistics	
Volunteers	Twice a month until one month out; then weekly	Email: Save the date, times, exciting news, logistics	Like a newsletter
All other Stakeholders	Weekly	Email	Project table (status)

Examples of frequency: daily, weekly, monthly, as needed

Examples of medium: email, report, presentation, drop in, meeting

Sidebar 2.9

Your Communications Plan

Use this table to brainstorm the best way to communicate with your stakeholders as the project progresses.

STAKEHOLDER	FREQUENCY	MEDIUM	COMMENTS
Sponsor			

However, project communication cannot take away from actually doing the project. If you communicate too frequently, people will stop listening to you. Build a communications plan that is effective and minimal. You can't afford too much or too little.

Strategies for Influencing Stakeholders

Here are some quick tips for communicating effectively during a project (there will be more in Chapter 4, "Manage"):

- When delivering bad or difficult news, the first communication should not be email. It should be face-to-face if at all possible, with a phone call being the second best.

- Whom you include is critical, and equally important is whom you do not include. Often it is better to include a particular person to build collaboration, even if you don't think his or her role really merits this level of attention. More is better.

- "More is better" seems to conflict with the approach of minimizing communication noted above, but as you will see in Chapter 4 ("Manage"), it is easy to include multiple stakeholders in brief, frequent communication. Adding another email address doesn't add work.

CREATING A GOVERNANCE PLAN (CHANGE MANAGEMENT)

At the start of a project, it's very easy for everyone to get along. Nothing is happening yet. At a recent meeting someone said to me, "We've always been in a team culture here, and we do it very well. We don't need leaders; we all lead." This is a great thing at the start of a project, but as the project progresses, decision making will be very slow if it is being done by more than one person. While you still have the political power, sketch out a plan for how changes will be prioritized once the project starts. Exhibit 2.19 shows a template for the kinds of choices you must make. This governance plan (also sometimes called change management) will be the go-to process as insurance against serious conflicts and politics disrupting your project when it is in progress.

Who Should Be Involved?

Exhibit 2.19 shows you who should be involved during the determination and sharing of your governance plan.

Exhibit 2.19

ARCI* Governance Plan

	PROJECT SPONSOR	PROJECT MANAGER	STAKEHOLDERS
Determine the governance plan for types of project changes.	INFORMED/ CONSULTED	ACCOUNTABLE/ RESPONSIBLE	INFORMED/ CONSULTED
Share the governance plan with appropriate stakeholders.	INFORMED/ CONSULTED	ACCOUNTABLE/ RESPONSIBLE	INFORMED/ CONSULTED

*ARCI: ACCOUNTABLE: the buck stops here. RESPONSIBLE: does the task. CONSULTED: shares expertise. INFORMED: told about the task.

Technique: Governance Plan

The governance plan is really a modified ARCI table for changes that will occur to scope (requirements, number of stakeholders, size, processes, and technology), budget, and schedule.

In Exhibit 2.20, notice the escalation metric described in the criteria column. The project manager on the Day of Caring project is going to make small decisions (up to $1000 and two weeks of variation on the calendar) and will "escalate" to the project sponsor for anything over that. Notice also that some stakeholders, for example, the catering manager, are expected to manage their own variance in their own way.

Use the table in Sidebar 2.10 to establish decision-making criteria for your project.

Exhibit 2.20

Governance Plan: Day of Caring Project

TYPE OF CHANGE	CRITERIA	RESPONSIBLE	ACCOUNTABLE	CONSULTED	INTERESTED
Requirements (more/less scope, change in existing risk factors)	Impact < two weeks' calendar time+; budget increase < $1000	Project manager	Project manager	Project sponsor	Stakeholders
Requirements (more/less scope, change in existing risk factors)	Impact > two weeks' calendar time; budget increase > $1000	Project sponsor	Project manager	Stakeholders	
Catering changes	Impact > $500	Project manager	Catering manager		
. . . etc.					

"+" assumes that there is an extra two weeks in the schedule prior to the event date.

Accountable: the buck stops here. Responsible: does the task. Consulted: shares expertise. Informed: told about the task.

Potential Challenges

It would be impressive if your governance plan stayed constant for your project, but that is very unlikely. Although it is important to create a governance plan early in your project, while everyone is willing to talk about it calmly, it is also likely that roles will change during a project, as will the governance plan.

COMPLETING A DRAFT PROJECT CHARTER

Before moving on, take a minute to audit your project charter for completeness. Sidebar 2.11 will provide you with criteria to make sure you are not rushing through this extremely important deliverable.

Reusing Your Project Charter

Depending on the field that you are in, you will tend to do projects that are somewhat similar over and over again. One of the great things about doing a project charter is that the next time you do a project you can often simply modify the charter you have already created. For example, I do a lot of course development projects. No matter which course I am developing, I always have a customer or customer sponsor, subject matter experts, proposed audience (students), graphic designers, and so on. It saves me a lot of time to begin with an existing scope diagram and change it rather than start from scratch. Business objectives and project objectives may also be similar. It's also a great help to read risks I've had in the past to remind me of things I might have forgotten.

Software Options

I am not a big proponent of using complicated software for the project charter. In fact, the snazzier it looks, the more likely people won't challenge what you've documented. Remember, we want bad news early. I actually keep my scope diagrams on flipcharts, but where you work, that might not be possible or appropriate. Instead, consider hand-drawing and scanning the scope diagram. You can use PowerPoint, Visio, or any other graphic program to draw these diagrams, but again I caution you not to get too professional with them. Remember, the project charter is *always* a draft.

For the other documents (business and project objectives, risk, constraints, communications plan, governance plan), I use Word or Excel. Many of our customers like to organize these files in a web community or SharePoint so they can share them as a project team.

 Lou's Project Management Diary

A large U.S. pharmaceutical company took an interesting approach to sponsorship and governance, which paid off down the road. When beginning a project for a global ERP system, the executives, led by the CEO, chose a senior project manager to manage the project. This project manager was then responsible for choosing the project sponsor from the executive committee, someone who would have the political firepower needed to get the "Risk Average = 10" project completed successfully. The executive chosen would have his or her bonus money tied to project results. As this project progressed, incredible challenges emerged, including an acquisition that in midstream changed the selected software; a serious illness; and a serious recession. The project had plenty of challenges but has progressed forward impressively.

In this chapter, you have worked through the minimal documents and, more important, the thinking that will help you start a project well to end well. It isn't unusual, when this phase is "complete," to feel exhausted and reluctant to revisit any of it. Remind yourself that this is just the very start, and the hard work is yet to come—finishing the project.

Working on and discussing the project charter (definition) with as many stakeholders as possible is a great experience. Sharing all the learning about everyone else's perspectives is powerful. But be careful to keep the process moving. Work hard to sketch the entire set of documents out in less than an hour. You are creating a *draft*, not a *final* document. Remember, there is no way it can be a final document, because the project will continue to change as it progresses. This is a line drawn in the sand, a conversation that will continue. Continue to manage this expectation for your stakeholders.

SUMMARY CHECKLIST

In this chapter you learned how to:

- Create a project charter (definition) in 45 minutes to jump-start the project and mitigate against rework and chaos

- Determine why the project is being done, using the "Greek goddess" IRACIS: how will the project Increase Revenue, Avoid Cost, and/or Improve Service?

- Clarify the roles of project manager, sponsor, and stakeholders using an ARCI (Accountable, Responsible, Consulted, Informed) table

- Create a visual scope diagram with stakeholders, inputs, and outputs

- Do Quick and Dirty Risk Assessment and determine how to mitigate serious risks that could occur on your project

- Establish the constraints of the project

- Create a communications plan for all stakeholders involved during the project

- Create a governance plan (change management) to document who will prioritize different types of change requests

CHAPTER 3

Plan

"Now that we're organized, what do we do?"

In this chapter, you will:

- Create a project schedule by adding up all the tasks (duration)
- Create due dates for project tasks by working back from the due date
- Leverage the scope diagram to determine milestones
- Determine the tasks required for each milestone
- Determine the task dependencies
- Determine the resource dependencies, especially the people
- Incorporate risk mitigation and the communications plan into the project schedule
- Choose the best tool for the project schedule

Projects that have not been defined weigh heavily on your brain. Many of us have great wish lists—strategic projects that we know will improve our organization and that we also know will take more time than we have right now. These projects nag us and worry us. It's very hard to do strategic work when you are already feeling overwhelmed.

In Chapter 2 ("Define"), you learned how to get a project off on the right foot by creating visual documents of the following conversations:

- Business objectives (IRACIS)
- Scope diagram
- Project objectives
- Risks and mitigation
- Constraints
- Governance plan
- Communications plan

If you are jumping to this phase without completing the Define phase, four side effects will likely doom your success:

1. It is very likely that you will leave out a large chunk of work (for a missing stakeholder) since this phase involves detailed work that will determine the scope of the project and the creation of a project schedule.

2. You'll end up with an overly expansive project scope since you won't have clarity about why the project is being done (the business objectives).

3. You'll have some brutal surprises in "Manage" (Chapter 4) since you built no risk mitigation into your project plan.

4. You'll have to add time to your project later on because you didn't build in any time for communications; as a bonus you will succeed in alienating your stakeholders.

The project management model that I introduced in Chapter 1 consists of these four phases:

Define answers the question *why*

Plan answers the question *how*

Manage requires seeking to *adapt*

Review requires seeking to *learn*

The model is repeated in Exhibit 3.1, but with the bullets of the major deliverables of the Plan phase. This chapter will focus on *Plan* ("Properly" in the parlance of our catchy phrase, "Dare to Properly Manage Resources").

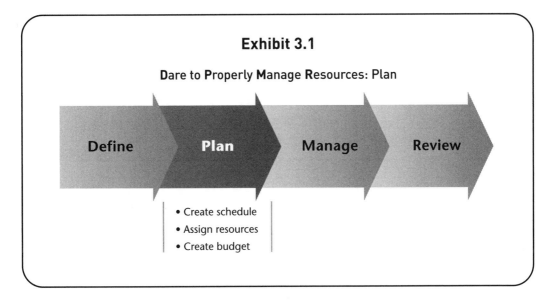

Exhibit 3.1

Dare to Properly Manage Resources: Plan

Define — Plan — Manage — Review

• Create schedule
• Assign resources
• Create budget

CREATING THE PROJECT PLAN

The Plan phase contains steps with visual techniques for answering, from multiple angles, the question:

How can I bring the right people, resources, and tasks together to meet the business objectives for this project?

Plan explores *how* the project will be done. It is the strategy that you, as expert project manager, will create to complete a successful project. Strategies by nature are guesses. No one (including you) can anticipate the future with any accuracy, so when you build a project plan, it is very likely that it will change somewhere along the road. This document is the road map: it helps everyone involved understand what they are supposed to be doing and when it has to be done so that the project will stay on schedule.

A good project plan frees up the project manager's time. If no master plan exists, the project manager ends up continually answering questions and helping everyone involved remember what they are supposed to be working on, what the deliverable is, and when the various parts of the project are due.

This can be very frustrating. It creates a perception in the project manager that no one is responsible and accountable. That may be true to some extent, but it is more likely that in the chaos of a typical day in the office, the project team members may miss a deadline or fail to deliver on some promise.

Your investment in the Define phase really pays off now. You likely had some difficult conversations to create your *project charter* and set of deliverables; this is a decent jump start on creating your project plan. Imagine trying to create a project plan without having any idea of your project's ultimate outcome! This happens all the time, and is one of the biggest mistakes in project management. It is so tempting to immediately start figuring out dates on a calendar when asked to do an important project. You can pretty much bet on the calendar being wrong if you've left out Define.

The *business objectives* also are important to keep in mind as you build the project plan. Business objectives help you keep your perspective and remind you to always ask the question, "Why is the business doing this project?" The scope diagram helps you determine what needs to be done, in two ways. First, it allows your stakeholders to help you brainstorm the milestones of the project (a *milestone* is a big chunk of related tasks that contribute to something important being done by a certain date). Second, the arrows flowing in and out of your scope diagram help you clearly identify the work that needs to be done. (We'll go into more detail on this later in this chapter.)

The *project objectives* clarify how you measure the completion of key project deliverables. This is a great sanity check. Auditing your project plan against your project objectives ensures you've thought of all the work to be done, including testing and training activities, which are often forgotten until the last minute and then not done well. Similarly, the *project constraints* decision made in Define is a good audit for evaluating whether you've developed the best strategy for your unique project. For example, are you creating a plan that focuses on speed, when cost is really the most important factor? *Risk mitigation* activities require work and must be scheduled for them to actually get done. The *communications plan* also requires work that potentially shows up on the plan.

It is very common to discover new stakeholders and project flows while building a plan. Depending on your *governance plan*, you may have to go back to the project sponsor to approve the scope changes. Remember, the project charter is a living conversation, changing and evolving just like your project. Your project plan also has a flexible structure. You must be willing to change your plan when the situation demands a change. Insanity happens, and it has nothing to do with your talent as a project manager. Poor project managers pretend the world never changes, but you know better.

The Project Management Institute (PMI) standard terminology identifies elements of project management differently from how I do. PMI methodology includes what I call the *project charter* and *project schedule* under the umbrella of *project plan*. I use the term *project plan* to mean just the *project schedule* for the purposes of this book as a way to emphasize the different natures of the terms. Therefore, I use *project plan* to define the deliverables of the Plan phase.

The project plan is the project manager's primary job. As project manager, you are accountable for getting the project done; the buck stops with you. You might think of the plan as your map for the future. You might still get lost, though.

DETERMINING THE MILESTONES AND THEIR DUE DATES

In the process of managing projects, most of us more easily visualize project milestones. For example, when you start your work day, you think about what you need to complete. We don't really think too much about how many steps are involved to get the milestone done. For many it is much easier to figure out milestones first, and then figure out how to get them done with tasks. Again, if you'd prefer to start with tasks, move on to the next section, "Identifying the Project Tasks."

A milestone is *when* you think some big chunk of work will be completely done. It's a line in the sand. In a project, there are usually multiple milestones and a certain order in which they have to be done. Exhibit 3.2 shows the milestones surrounding the scope diagram for our Day of Caring project. Exhibit 3.3 shows the order of the milestones. Some milestones happen successively. For example, the milestone "Catering Contract Signed" has to occur before milestone "Food Delivered to Site."

Exhibit 3.2

Milestones: Day of Caring Project

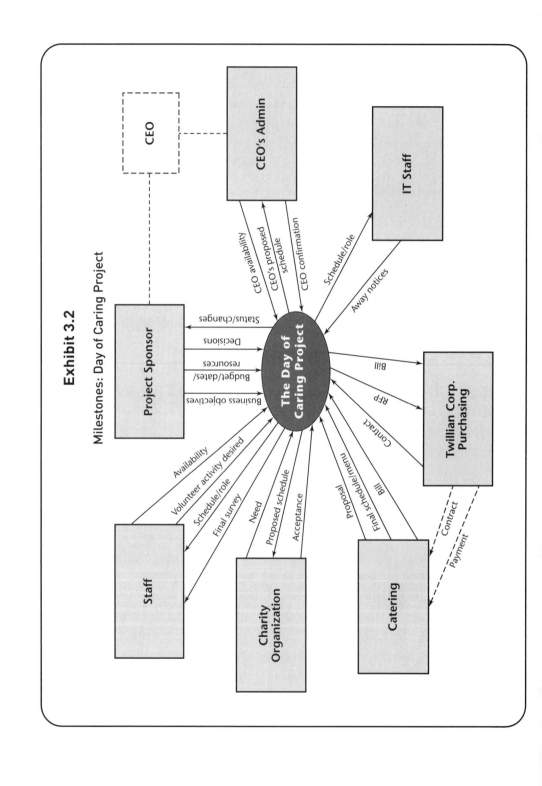

Remember, milestones don't take time. Milestones are just completion dates along the road to a required deliverable. In the next section you'll learn how to differentiate between a task and a milestone. To make sure you begin to get the difference right now, do the following: write out your milestones with a *noun* plus a *verb* (in past tense). Here are a few examples:

Testing completed

Requirements approved

Transition finished

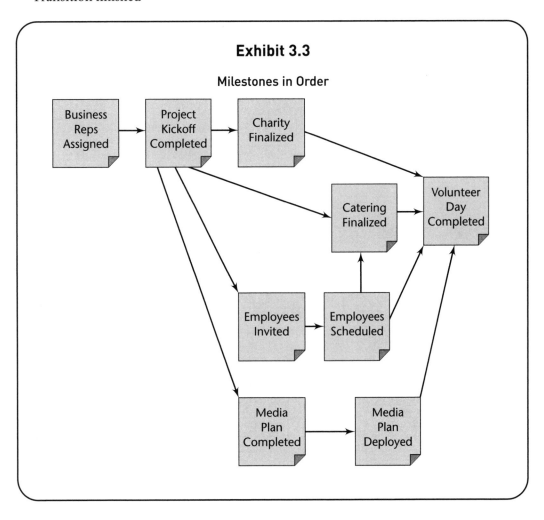

Exhibit 3.3

Milestones in Order

Notice how naming them this way reminds you that a milestone is the *end* of a series of tasks, not the beginning. This is not a common exercise, but I highly encourage you to perform it so that you won't mix yourself up when you work back from ambitious dates.

For very small projects, milestones are overkill and you should skip straight to tasks.

Who Should Be Involved?

In all the steps and techniques discussed in this chapter, the roles involved will be primarily the same. They are listed in Exhibit 3.4.

Exhibit 3.4

ARCI* Roles: Planning Phase

	PROJECT SPONSOR	PROJECT MANAGER	STAKEHOLDERS
Determine the milestones.	INFORMED	ACCOUNTABLE/ RESPONSIBLE	CONSULTED
Determine the tasks and task dependencies within the milestones.		ACCOUNTABLE/ RESPONSIBLE	CONSULTED
Determine the resources available and the resource dependencies.		ACCOUNTABLE/ RESPONSIBLE	CONSULTED
Incorporate risk management tasks and constraints into the schedule.		ACCOUNTABLE/ RESPONSIBLE	INFORMED
Choose and implement the best tool for your project schedule.	INFORMED	ACCOUNTABLE/ RESPONSIBLE	INFORMED

*ARCI: ACCOUNTABLE: the buck stops here. RESPONSIBLE: does the task. CONSULTED: shares expertise. INFORMED: told about the task.

Technique: Project Milestones

Here are three ways I figure out my project milestones:

1. Take a look at each stakeholder on the scope diagram (Exhibit 2.5) and follow this procedure:

   - Think about what value each delivers to the project.

   - Write the value as one or more milestones. In our example, the catering company might have two milestones—"Catering Contract Signed" and "Food Delivered to Site." I often write these on Post-its and place them on a white board or flipchart copy of the scope diagram. The activity flowing from the stakeholder to the project center will help you think through the big chunks of value the stakeholder will deliver. Not all the work within this milestone will be done by the stakeholder, but some of it will.

   - Next look at the flows going from the project center to the stakeholders. This is the work that has to be done by the project team. For example, you might have a milestone such as "RFPs Sent," and you'll use that milestone to create a list of work that needs to be done.

   - When you've looked at each stakeholder and work flow, complete the puzzle. Put the milestones in the order that makes sense; this is easy to do with Post-its. Indicate any milestones that you can do concurrently as the last step.

2. This technique works best if you've done a similar project before. Read your project objectives and scan your scope diagram one more time. Take out a blank piece of paper and write down a sequential, high-level list of what needs to be done. Use your intuition and your experiences to figure it out from beginning to end. It may help to convert your list to Post-its at some point so you can make sure the sequencing is correct. Indicate any milestones that can be done concurrently as the last step.

3. Start with the phases of the methodology your organization uses to develop training, systems, new products, clinical trials, or whatever it is your project is going to deliver. Use the scope diagram to validate that

you have all the milestones you need for your specific project. Most development methodologies are built around a basic problem-solving model:

- Research and analyze the problem or opportunity
- Design a solution
- Build the solution
- Transition to the solution
- Evaluate the solution

For example, Exhibit 3.5 shows the traditional phases of developing a new training class. Exhibit 3.6 shows a methodology for developing an IT system. Exhibit 3.7 shows a new product development methodology. The advantage

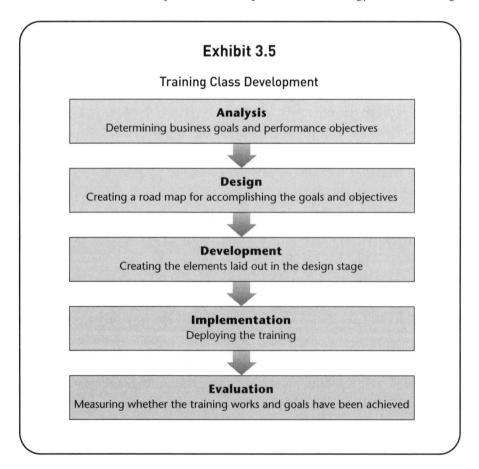

Exhibit 3.5

Training Class Development

Analysis
Determining business goals and performance objectives

Design
Creating a road map for accomplishing the goals and objectives

Development
Creating the elements laid out in the design stage

Implementation
Deploying the training

Evaluation
Measuring whether the training works and goals have been achieved

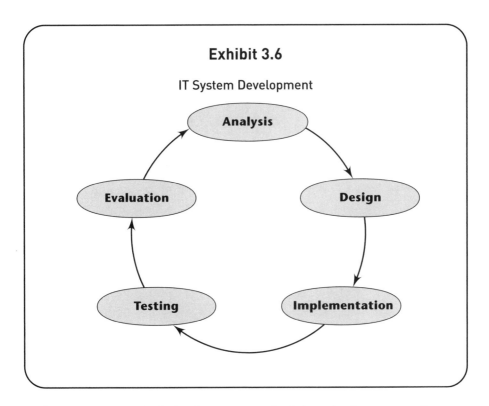

Exhibit 3.6

IT System Development

of following a standard development methodology is that your milestones (which are generally the phases) and your tasks are all spelled out for you—no brainstorming required. These traditional approaches to development have been labeled "waterfall methodologies," meaning you complete one phase before you start the next, which of course is never true. The world doesn't stop while you are doing your project, so it's natural for things to change while the project progresses. This has led to the development of a similar yet different approach to projects, called the Agile approach.

First adopted by software developers and more recently by online course developers, the Agile approach is similar to traditional methodologies in the following way:

- The milestones are still analyze, design, develop, and implement
- Project management is still critical
- Very specific roles and governance are defined
- Communication is an imperative

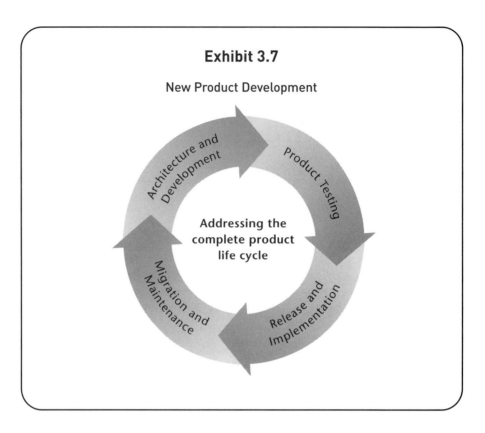

Exhibit 3.7

New Product Development

Architecture and Development

Product Testing

Addressing the complete product life cycle

Migration and Maintenance

Release and Implementation

Agile is a different approach. Rather than do the *whole* project in a waterfall method, the approach breaks a project into features—things the customer wants. The project is broken into small, quick projects (called "scrums"). The customer decides which features it wants in each cycle. Other key differences include:

- The project team is dedicated as much as possible to the project, and the customers are available whenever they are needed. This collaborative partnership is key to the success of these "SWAT" team scrums.

- Although there is a front-end scope of the whole project, this evolves as the scrums continue. As new things are learned by the customers and developers, change occurs frequently. In fact, change is expected.

- Developers track their "velocity" and get better at estimating what they can really get done as the cycles continue. Customers are asked to pick features that can be done based on this velocity.

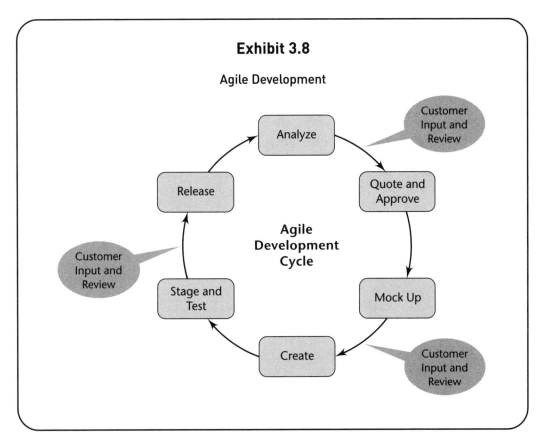

Exhibit 3.8

Agile Development

Analyze

Customer Input and Review

Quote and Approve

Agile Development Cycle

Mock Up

Release

Customer Input and Review

Stage and Test

Create

Customer Input and Review

Agile is not the same as prototyping. Prototyping is a way to test a design, and a prototype is not a fully functional, operational deliverable. Using the Agile approach, each cycle ("scrum") delivers a fully functional "thing" to the client, which it can use immediately. Exhibit 3.8 shows a graphic that illustrates this approach. Notice that the idea of a project being finished is missing. Theoretically—and difficult in practice—the project is finished when the customer says it is. This is not explicit in the beginning.

Let's go back to your project. Think about the three approaches above and try each one on your project. Sidebar 3.1 will help you experiment with these different approaches.

Regardless of which technique you use, the last thing to do is a sanity check. Reread your business and project objectives. Now look at the milestones you have created. Do they make sense? Have you forgotten anything? Have you included risk mitigation and communication planning?

Exhibit 3.9 shows the milestones with dates. These were created by working back from the due date. Rarely do we get a project anymore that comes with an open end date, so get comfortable with doing this for your project. Use Sidebar 3.2 to do just that.

IDENTIFYING THE PROJECT TASKS

A widely known technique for planning by task in traditional project management is the Work Breakdown Structure (WBS). Work Breakdown Structures are a hierarchical way of brainstorming the tasks that will be needed to meet your business and project objectives. You start with the big chunks of activities that must be done and break each down until at the lowest level you are at a task level. Each branch does not have to break down to the same number of levels. Milestones are created from one of the levels above the tasks.

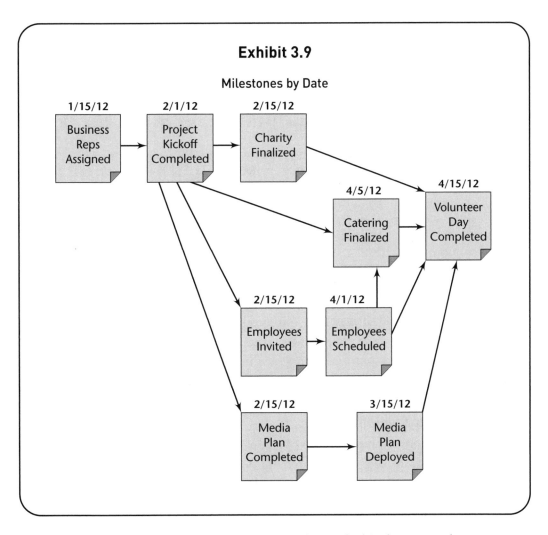

Exhibit 3.9

Milestones by Date

| 1/15/12 | 2/1/12 | 2/15/12 |
| Business Reps Assigned | Project Kickoff Completed | Charity Finalized |

4/5/12
Catering Finalized

4/15/12
Volunteer Day Completed

2/15/12
Employees Invited

4/1/12
Employees Scheduled

2/15/12
Media Plan Completed

3/15/12
Media Plan Deployed

Exhibit 3.10 is an example of a WBS. Notice that with this document the work is top-down. Some people love this approach, while it confuses others. If you are using a WBS and it confuses you more than it helps, don't use it.

I suggest you try it now (Sidebar 3.3) on your project to see whether it's a tool that you will find useful.

Whether you . . .

- Brainstorm tasks top-down using a Work Breakdown Structure
- Sequentially build the tasks from start to finish
- Use your standard methodology to choose the tasks you think fit your project

... you will always miss some tasks. When you begin to sequence the tasks, you will likely discover new tasks. No worries—you'll discover new tasks throughout the entire project. Shoot for 80 percent and move on. Don't get paralyzed by the plan construction.

Potential Challenges

Building milestones that are too big to complete is a common problem. For example, a project with the milestones "All Killing Stopped" and "World at Peace" is probably at too high a level to be able to figure out how to get the project done.

A similar problem is skipping milestones entirely and trying to jump right into tasks, especially for a large project. If you are going to have more than twenty tasks on a project, you need to group them together with milestones just so your head is able to manage the complexity.

Another common challenge is getting started on this process. If this happens to you, take heart that you are not the first. Find a few other people who will exchange team brainstorming for a free cup of coffee.

Take another look at the milestones and tasks for your project. Go back to your scope diagram and read through the inputs and outputs (arrows). This is an early way to test the completeness of your task list. Sidebar 3.4 guides you through this review process.

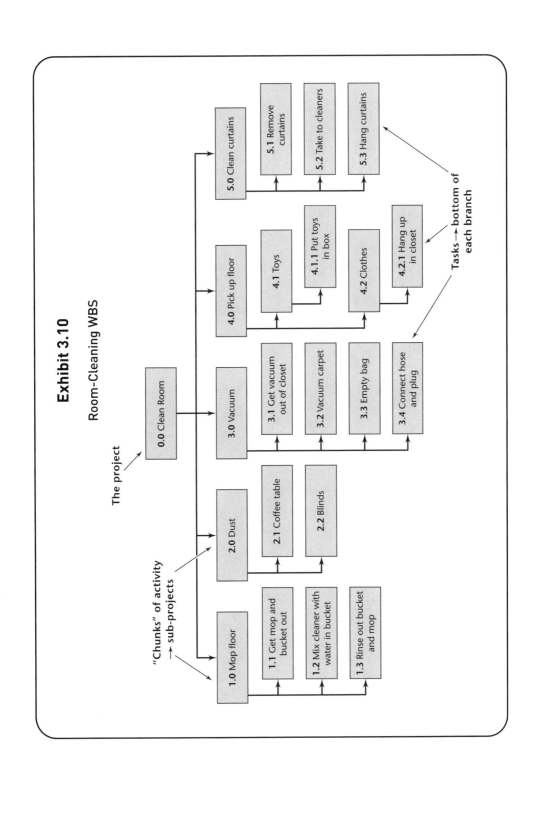

Exhibit 3.10

Room-Cleaning WBS

The project

0.0 Clean Room

"Chunks" of activity → sub-projects

1.0 Mop floor
- 1.1 Get mop and bucket out
- 1.2 Mix cleaner with water in bucket
- 1.3 Rinse out bucket and mop

2.0 Dust
- 2.1 Coffee table
- 2.2 Blinds

3.0 Vacuum
- 3.1 Get vacuum out of closet
- 3.2 Vacuum carpet
- 3.3 Empty bag
- 3.4 Connect hose and plug

4.0 Pick up floor
- 4.1 Toys
  - 4.1.1 Put toys in box
- 4.2 Clothes
  - 4.2.1 Hang up in closet

5.0 Clean curtains
- 5.1 Remove curtains
- 5.2 Take to cleaners
- 5.3 Hang curtains

Tasks → bottom of each branch

Sidebar 3.3

Trying a WBS on Your Project

Work Breakdown Structures (WBS) are a hierarchical way of brainstorming the tasks that will be needed to meet your business and project objectives. You start with the big "chunks" of activities that must be done and break them down until at the lowest level you are at a task level. Notice that branches do not have to break down to the same number of levels. This blank chart is used as a starting point for you to try it on your own project, but it's easier if you use Visio, PowerPoint SmartArt, or some other common software to build these.

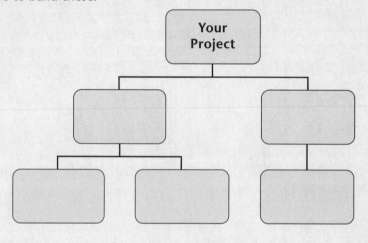

Sidebar 3.4

Reviewing Your Milestones and Tasks

Return to the project charter that you created in the last chapter for your project. Revisit the business objectives, read through your scope diagram, and look at your project objectives. Do your milestones *really* represent the big chunks of work that need to be done for your project to be successful? Are there arrows on your scope diagram that really don't fit and need their own milestone? Have all the project objectives been accounted for?

Take some time with this. Missing pieces discovered *now* are much less costly than missing pieces that have to be forced in when discovered during user or final testing.

At some point you will face tasks that are actually shared by more than one milestone. Usually that means that the milestones aren't detailed enough, and it may make sense to break them down a bit to avoid confusing crossover between tasks. Another option is to make a bigger milestone and combine all the tasks under a single milestone.

Strategies for Influencing Stakeholders

For the most part, the person you are most influencing in this process of identifying tasks is yourself. Honoring your own unique needs for processing is the first step.

Creating a project plan is a problem-solving activity. You are taking something big and trying to figure out how to break it down into smaller pieces. Nobody really cares how you get to the small pieces, and unlike your experience in school, you don't have to show your work. Give yourself permission to solve your project "problem" with a technique that helps your brain the most. Once you get the schedule done, you don't need to keep your brainstorming notes.

Howard Gardner, a Harvard University learning and development expert, has researched how people process problems through his Multiple Intelligences (for more information on this, see my book *The Accelerated Learning Fieldbook*). We all think in unique ways because each of our brains is unique. Gardner initially determined seven ways people process information, including what you'll see in Exhibit 3.11.

In 1987, Gardner suggested three additional intelligences:

- Emotional: you are aware of emotions and regulate; you work in an uninterrupted space
- Naturalistic: nature calls you—you take outside breaks, work near windows
- Existential: you have a sense of purpose; you trust your instincts

You will read more about Emotional Intelligence (EQ) in the next chapter when you learn how to mitigate your stress level to improve decision making.

Exhibit 3.11

Gardner's Multiple Intelligences

INTELLIGENCE	CHARACTERISTIC	PLANNING STYLE
Intrapersonal	thinking alone	Make your best guess by yourself before sharing with others
Linguistic/Verbal	written or spoken word	Discuss with others or write words on Post-its
Spatial/Visual	in pictures	Mind Maps or Post-its on the wall
Musical	listening to music (or singing)	Play instrumental music to help focus
Logical-mathematical	analytical, stepwise	Work by step: WBS, milestone/task, this/then, MS Project
Interpersonal	thinking with others	Work with a group
Bodily-kinesthetic	movement and emotion	Post-its on a wall, Mind Map (software)

DETERMINING THE TASK DEPENDENCIES

I call this step "Pants, Then Shoes"—that is, there are tasks that cannot be started until another task is done. There are also tasks that can be done virtually anytime, and tasks that can be done at the same time if you have enough people to work on them. Figuring out the task dependencies allows you to accurately schedule the tasks and determine how many people it will take to get the project done as quickly as possible.

In Chapter 1 you learned that a task is a small unit of work, with a beginning and end. The technique you used to figure out the milestones will also work for figuring out the tasks. Some people like to brainstorm by creating piles of Post-its with all the tasks that need to occur to complete a milestone;

then they sequence the Post-its. Some people would rather brainstorm tasks sequentially from start to finish for each milestone. Pick what works best for you. A combination of both is also useful for some people.

Technique: Task Dependencies

Think of this technique as gluing milestones and tasks together. It's like a giant puzzle, so Post-its or Post-it software work well. Use a specific color Post-it for milestones and another for tasks, so you can keep them straight. Create two new milestones, "Project Started" and "Project Ended."

Using a large wall, place your "Project Started" Post-it to the far left and "Project Ended" Post-it to the far right. Put your other milestones in between these in the order you already figured out. Next put the tasks that are required to complete each milestone to the left of the milestone. This can be a little confusing, so remember that the milestone indicates that all the tasks are *done*, so the tasks must happen prior to (to the left of) the milestone.

Now "sew" them all together. Basically, your job is to draw arrows from the first task to the next, and so on. If you were following a strict PMI methodology approach, you'd be starting a Critical Path Diagram, but that is more complex than you need for smaller projects. You are simply trying to figure out where on the calendar these tasks' due dates will fall. If you want to get really creative and you're doing this as a team, cut small pieces of string or yarn and put them between tasks that have task dependencies, or use Post-it flags.

Some people like to use large sheets of butcher-block paper on the wall and draw arrows with pencils first, then with marker. Others like to use various color Post-its for arrows. Exhibit 3.12 shows a partial view of the task dependencies from our case study. It is okay to have multiple arrows coming out of your Post-it tasks. In fact, it's very common to have interdependent tasks.

When you've figured out all your task dependencies, revisit the tasks that aren't connected, either coming out toward another task or coming in from one. Even if a task doesn't have other dependencies, it must be completed between the start and end milestones. When you are done, every task should have at least one arrow (or string) coming into it and one coming out, connecting that task to either another task or a milestone.

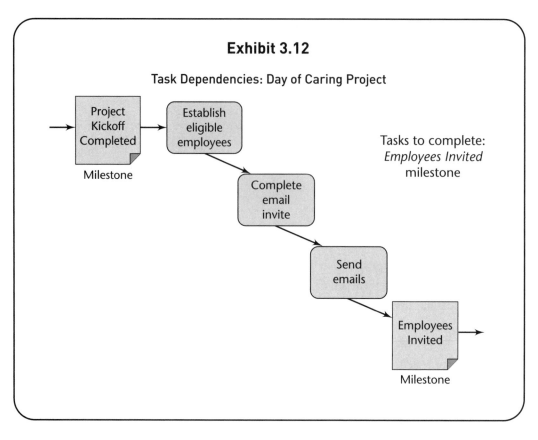

Exhibit 3.12

Task Dependencies: Day of Caring Project

Project Kickoff Completed
Milestone

Establish eligible employees

Complete email invite

Send emails

Employees Invited
Milestone

Tasks to complete:
Employees Invited
milestone

You may have some tasks such as "Sign the contract" for which you could make the case that every task depends on "Sign the contract." It would look horribly busy to draw a dependency from "Sign the contract" to every other task in the plan, although it is technically accurate. Instead, if the next task is "Choose volunteers," and we know that "Train volunteers" is obviously dependent on "Choose volunteers" (which was dependent on "Sign the contract"), then by default we've shown that "Train volunteers" is also dependent on "Sign the contract." Exhibit 3.13 shows both examples. It's always a good idea to reduce complexity when possible.

Strategies for Influencing Stakeholders

In Chapter 1, I warned you about the danger of confusing a task with large deliverables that take multiple people to complete. However, depending on the

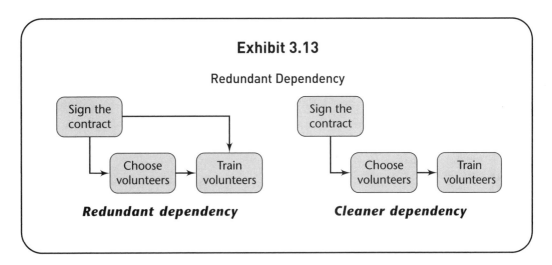

Exhibit 3.13

Redundant Dependency

Redundant dependency

Cleaner dependency

size of your project, you might create a list of tasks that break the rules about what a task is and what a project is.

If a large group of tasks is going to be completely done by a stakeholder, and there's no need to track any other handoffs, it's better to list it as a task, although clearly it breaks all the rules of a task that we began the book with. For example, if you have a stakeholder in the IT group who is going to build a temporary, shared web portal to share a volunteer schedule, you could have a task that says "Build web portal volunteer schedule." There are two good reasons for actually leaving the detail out: (1) it makes the schedule a little simpler to read, and (2) it ensures that everyone is perfectly clear that no one else is involved in this task. Many times project managers try to guess the tasks for a set of project tasks that they don't have expertise to do. Either ask the IT resource to tell you the tasks, or make one big task and hold them accountable for delivering it.

On the other hand, there are times when you want to have a few extra checkpoints in a completely outsourced group of tasks just to make sure they stay on track—maybe because they usually don't. One of my customers taught me, "You can't expect what you don't inspect." If it's important that it be done on time, don't just check on it on the due date.

For example, if one of your tasks is to make sure that an external vendor delivers food to an event, you may wish to put in a couple of tasks prior to "Pick up food." Clearly, it makes sense to also have tasks like "Submit menu,"

"Approve menu," and so on. Notice how I haven't tried to take over the job of the caterer; I'm just trying to be clear enough to be able to track progress.

At this point in the process, you may very well be working alone or with a small team. Stakeholders and your project sponsors are not interested in doing this work; they just want it done. The process takes a long time, a lot of brain power, and may be confusing at times.

Moreover, you and your team may be tired of the work. But you are not finished just yet.

You have more work to do, including figuring out who is working on each task and how much effort each task will take. And just as important, you still don't have enough information to figure out when the project will be done.

DETERMINING THE RESOURCE (PEOPLE) DEPENDENCIES

Recently, I hired a new person to help us on a project who did not have the technical skills required. I didn't think these skills would be a big deal to teach. What I relearned is that sometimes teaching the skills is counterproductive and gets in the way of the project moving forward. People with the skills required to do a task take less time than people with less skills. This is pretty obvious, but we often underestimate the impact, including the time taken away from other project resources to get the new person up to speed.

Similarly, even a person with the right skills will struggle without business knowledge. One of our customers had a tendency to move their best and brightest project managers to struggling projects. This constant reallocation neutralized the project management skills of the previously successful superstar, because the project manager never had time to learn the business context of each project. Those with business knowledge will complete tasks more quickly than a person without that knowledge.

In this resource step, think about who will be working on each task and how their business knowledge and technical skills will impact the duration of the task. Instead of asking, "How long will this task take?" try asking this question: "How long will this task take if a specific person is assigned the task?" You'll likely get two different answers.

It's time for you to try it. After you've determined your tasks and dependencies and hooked them all together between start and end, it's time to assign one task owner to each task. This reinforces accountability, as you've just read. Use Sidebar 3.5 to work through this thought process.

This can be an eye-opening activity. Many people complete their project schedule before they know who will be working on the tasks. Obviously, that's going to challenge the likelihood of meeting the dates you promise.

Sidebar 3.5

Tasks and Owners

Go back to your tasks and assign *one* name to every task. This person is responsible and accountable for getting the task done. While the person assigned may get help from others, his or her skills and knowledge will greatly influence how much time it takes to complete the task. Ask yourself the following questions:

- What types of skills will this task require? Does this person have these skills?

- What types of business knowledge will this task require? Does this person know these things?

If you can't answer these questions with any confidence, it may be necessary to talk with the person you're thinking of assigning the task to before deciding who the best person for each task is.

In the real world, you are often stuck with whoever has been assigned to the task, so learning the answers to these questions just helps you estimate more effectively.

Lack of Resources

You may also have some new dependencies because of a lack of resources. Tasks that you decided could be done concurrently may have to be done one at a time because they are being done by the same person. Depending on the size of your project, you may be the only resource on the project, or nearly the only resource. In this case, parallel tasks are impossible: you have to show tasks realistically on your project schedule as happening one after the other. It's possible then for two tasks to not have any task dependency, but one task may be waiting for another to finish because no one else is available to work on it.

Potential Challenges

Some of the people you assign tasks to will likely be stakeholders. Stakeholders are responsible for any work implied by the arrows on the scope diagram that go from a stakeholder box to the project center. Sometimes new project managers mistakenly believe that they need to do all the tasks, or don't consider including the tasks done by others on the project schedule.

In fact, tasks done by stakeholders are the most difficult to manage. Most tasks today fall into this category. In general, the project manager has no formal authority to make a stakeholder finish a task. Often the stakeholder has a full plate at work and has no room for this additional work. Tasks being done by stakeholders should be considered riskier, increasing the likelihood that the task will be late. When estimating the time for these tasks (in the next section), consider the skills and business knowledge of the stakeholder, but make sure you allow for the fact that this work will be done in addition to the stakeholder's full-time job.

As you go through the tasks, you may find a needed skill set that requires training. If you think this training makes sense, don't forget that it will add more work to the project. If it's necessary work and was not included in the original scope, consider at a minimum building tasks for the training. You might even go back and add arrows to your scope diagram.

Strategies for Influencing Stakeholders

The sooner you let people know the work that will be required and when that work is due, the better your chances are to lead a successful project. Good sales techniques are an important part of successful project work, as is keeping the information flowing from Day One. As you learned in the last chapter, let as many people as possible know about your project charter—and the sooner the better. Your completed project schedule will also be a critical shared document to minimize the conflict inherent in project task completion and handoff.

If you have any questions about who will be working on your project, their skill sets, or their business knowledge, ask right up front. Although these conversations may be difficult—especially if the people don't even know they are among your project stakeholders—this early intervention will pay real dividends later.

FINALIZING TASK DUE DATES

Here's a modern-day reality. Most project assignments (no matter when they were assigned) come with a due date. Good or bad, this is an organizational reality. The technique I outline below reflects this reality.

Let's review before we go on. You have figured out:

- The milestones and the dates by when they have to be completed
- How to sew the tasks together in a way that is mindful of the task dependencies
- Who will be responsible and accountable for each task

The last step is to figure out how long each task will take. All the work that you have done thus far culminates with this step and impacts the construction and management of the entire project timeline. After all, you are now working on the project dashboard.

If you've been doing the work in the sidebars, you have already assigned dates to the milestones of your project (or had them assigned to you). It's a math exercise from this point forward: all the tasks have to fit within the milestone dates, or you have to move the milestone dates. It all has to work together, or it's a lie.

It's tempting to confuse milestones with tasks and to spend time thinking about how long a milestone will take to complete. If the project is big enough to merit breaking it down into milestones, you cannot accurately estimate how long it will take to finish without breaking the milestones down into tasks; and each task that must be done to complete a milestone will take time. In the parlance of project management this is called *effort*. Effort answers the question "How long will this task take?" Essentially, effort is a measure of how long it might take an average person working uninterrupted to complete a task. As you learned in Chapter 1 when you were challenged to think differently about your to-do list, juggling multiple tasks and projects with constant interruptions is the norm. Reality is chaos. Effort doesn't matter; dates do.

This last phrase is extremely important to project management success. In reality, tasks are hardly ever done by an average person working uninterrupted. That's why we use another term—*duration*—to describe the way we actually work. Duration is sometimes called *elapsed time*.

Duration is reality; effort is wishful thinking. Duration is always longer than effort. The problem is that novice project managers mistakenly calculate when the project will be done using *effort* instead of *duration*. This mistake usually means the project will be late, most likely very late, before it even starts.

Two Approaches

The traditional project management approach, detailed in the PMBOK (Project Management Body of Knowledge), requires that you guess how long each task will take, inflating the number for weaker skill sets and business knowledge. For the schedule to be accurate, this timeline should reflect the translation of work effort (how long the task would take uninterrupted by an average individual) to duration (how long the task will take on the clock).

This is a tough, time-consuming approach. It also puts you in the position of estimating tasks to be done by stakeholders. Do you really have the skills to estimate these tasks? Since arriving at the estimates is all a guess, it's not unusual for the estimates to be off. If a project manager has never managed a similar project, this "guesstimate" is the only way forward.

The second approach, outlined below, is faster and more realistic. However, this approach requires that the project manager have some experience with a similar type of project. For example, if you were a trainer and were asked to manage a large e-learning rollout, you'd be forced to stick with a guessing approach.

Technique: Task Due Dates

Once you have come up with a list of tasks, and the tasks are linked together in order of their occurrence, and you know who will work on each task, it's time to assign real dates to the tasks. You start this process by beginning at the end of the project and working backwards.

You know the end due date. You've figured out a realistic date for each milestone to ensure the due date is met. Now work backwards through each milestone. Your job is to figure out the last possible day a task can be done so that you still stay on track to meet the project's overall due date. You are thinking backwards, so this takes a little getting used to.

Exhibit 3.14 shows the tasks for one of the milestones for the Day of Caring project. The question you use to figure this date out might be something like this: "If the 'Send emails' milestone has to be done by 2/15, then the task 'Complete email invite' must be done by 2/14, and the task 'Establish eligible employees' must be done by 2/7, . . ." and so on.

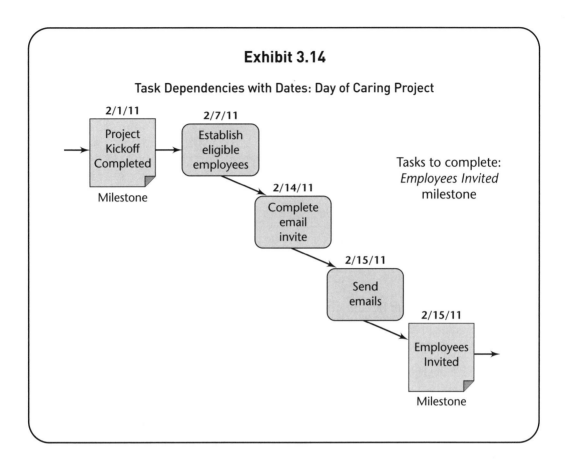

Exhibit 3.14

Task Dependencies with Dates: Day of Caring Project

2/1/11 — Project Kickoff Completed — Milestone

2/7/11 — Establish eligible employees

Tasks to complete:
Employees Invited
milestone

2/14/11 — Complete email invite

2/15/11 — Send emails

2/15/11 — Employees Invited — Milestone

Potential Challenges

This technique is very valuable for tasks that involve stakeholders. It relieves you of the responsibility of making estimates without the slightest bit of information. For stakeholders, the technique allows them latitude to take as much or as little time as they need so long as they hit the date. It's not a perfect arrangement since a stakeholder's task may have to wait until another task ends, or the date may be unrealistic. However, the methodology does offer some flexibility, since you send the project schedule with all the dates at the very start of the project. If necessary, you can negotiate new dates. You might even discover land mines that will make meeting your end date impossible.

Now it's your turn. It's time to roll up your sleeves and get your project plan to a task level with dates and task owners. Use Sidebar 3.6 to help you with this.

Strategies for Influencing Stakeholders

It's amazing how happy everyone will be about your project—the value it will bring, and your involvement—until you write *their* names on tasks with due dates. As you finish up your schedule, you will likely begin to get a sense of how committed your stakeholders are. At this point, you may see some additional organizational risk factors that may hinder the progress of your project. Write these potential roadblocks down with their risk factors. Don't worry about whether you feel comfortable sharing them with others. Consider what you will do now about possible delays and dropped balls.

PICKING THE BEST TOOL

Many people confuse project management software tools with project management. Project management is planning, organizing, and managing a project from start to end. Project management tools support *some* of this, but not all. For example, using Microsoft Project is not the same thing as managing your project, in the same way that using QuickBooks is not the same thing as running your business.

Your company may have picked a project management software package that you will be forced to use. If that's the case, then reading beyond this point may be pointless. Why? Because most project management software is tightly aligned to the PMBOK. And unfortunately, most software is really designed to support building the project schedule. Many of the most popular packages have no functions for building the project *charter*. This may be why so many people start projects with the schedule and skip thinking about why the project is being done—often a success-killing decision.

In 2008, PMI surveyed its members and found that the most-used project management software (85 percent) was Excel. Excel is the easiest way to build a project schedule, but it is difficult to represent task and resource dependencies with this tool. Microsoft Project keeps track of task and resource dependencies, tracks cost factors, and can be shared and summarized across entire companies. If you are on a large, enterprise-wide project, someone is most likely using Microsoft Project. However, the software tool is so powerful that it can be baffling to someone who doesn't need that complexity.

Software Alternatives

You can find other tools by surfing the Internet. Some tools are free, while others are inexpensive and still useful. You can also find tools that provide documentation management and discussion boards, which you can use during the building of your project charter. One of the biggest challenges of project management is managing the history of the email flow. A quick Google search will get you up to speed with the options available. You will also find tool reviews occasionally on the PMI website, but PMI members tend to be doing very large projects, so their perspective may be different from your own.

Regardless of the software tool you use, guard against the following:

- Do not let the tool take so much of your time that your project management suffers. If this happens, find an administrative person to do updates on the tool.

- Make the tool manage your project. Do not let the software confuse you with all kinds of bells and whistles you don't really need.

- Be cautious about the complexity of the reports, as well as the difficulty of printing. Giant maps of project tasks hurt heads. Don't hesitate to download the project into a simple spreadsheet and create your own reports from there.

- Don't force everyone to update their own tasks. This just adds overhead to people who already have too much to do, and aren't that excited about helping your project. Have them send their updates directly to you.

Lou's Project Management Diary

Customer Story

I am a big fan of the free online magazine called *ASK*, which is done by NASA (www.nasa.gov). In the stories and project reviews, NASA professionals share amazingly open stories about project lessons learned.

One article told the story of some NASA employees visiting a large company renowned for their project success. They were shown into a large meeting room, where project schedules were printed on large posters spanning entire walls, and charts and diagrams showed current status and other metrics. As we would be, the NASA professionals were duly impressed. They remarked about how amazing the room was. The guide shot them a quick look and told them, "Actually, these charts don't change very often. In fact, we just use this room to keep everyone off our backs while we get the project done."

The project schedule is a critical component to managing a project. If it is not read and kept up-to-date, the project manager has no other resource but to manage by the seat of his or her pants. This ensures that handouts will be missed, quality will suffer, and the project will likely struggle.

The purpose of creating the project plan is to know what needs to be done, who will do it, and when it will be done. Think of it as a dashboard for your project, helping you watch the speed, warning lights, and if you have GPS, your location. Your goal is to break down your milestones into the unique steps needed to get to those milestones. I use the term "task" to describe each of these steps. In the process, you brainstorm the tasks that you and the other project team members will need to do in order to check off a milestone. Eventually, each task you identify will have an owner and a due date.

By keeping this assignment of tasks in mind, you should be able to construct a reasonable level of detail. Ask the question, "Will this level of detail allow me to keep track of what's going on, and at the same time, is the detail big-picture enough so that I'm not micromanaging others?" It's a tricky balance, and you will likely make adjustments once the project starts. Most people make the tasks too big, but some spend way too much time breaking down every little step.

In this chapter, you have learned how to create a project schedule. It's fine to feel exhausted and reluctant to revisit this work after it's done. However, this is your project dashboard, and it has to be maintained, because it will change. Remember *flexible structure*: you have a plan, but you are open to changing the plan whenever reality dictates the need.

Once the project schedule is complete, share it with all the stakeholders and the project sponsor. Consider how much or little each group needs to see. In the next chapter, you will see how to convert your project schedule to a simple Excel spreadsheet, which will also work as your primary project communication tool.

SUMMARY CHECKLIST

In this chapter you learned how to:

- Identify the milestones for your project, working back from the project due date

- Identify each task that must be done to complete each milestone

- Identify any task dependencies; these are tasks that have to be completed before another can begin

- Identify any resource dependencies; these are tasks that can't be done concurrently, because only one person will be working on them

- Think about how the skills and business knowledge of a task owner will impact the time it will take to complete the task

- Establish the due date for each task, working back from the milestone due date

- Select a project management software tool that does what you need it to do, nothing more or less

- Prepare a project schedule to be the dashboard of your project so that it can begin and end successfully

CHAPTER 4

Manage

"It's not about how long the tasks will take. That's always a guess. It's about the drop-dead date."

In this chapter:

- Leverage the project plan to manage a project as it proceeds from start to end
- Use the deliverables of the project charter to keep the project from moving away from the business value it was planned to achieve
- Communicate project status effectively
- Influence stakeholders to stay accountable to on-time, on-budget deliverables by managing their expectations
- Diagnose negative emotions of those whose jobs will be changed by your projects
- Grow your own personal resiliency
- Learn more about your emotional competency and how your reaction to constant change impacts your decision making
- Leverage your behavioral strengths to learn to mitigate your emotional stress
- Leverage mental and physical techniques to prevent overwhelming stress

Lou's Project Management Diary

Years ago, I helped with the reorganization of a large IT group at a pharmaceutical company. The strategy was ahead of its time, arranging technical resources into "pools" that were "checked out" by projects. The hierarchy that had prevented innovation and speed was replaced by a new, more fluid and efficient model. Initially, the strategy was designed in secret meetings attended only by more senior or titled leaders—those with manager titles up to and including the chief information officer (CIO).

All this secrecy eventually created a sense of paranoia among the staff, who knew something was going on that they were not supposed to know about. Eventually, thanks to help from the organizational development staff, the managers decided some transparency was called for, and so a large poster with the entire reorganization roll-out schedule was posted in a common employee area. Everyone was invited to offer comments on a board. The idea was that more transparency would reduce fear and confusion in the company.

A manager responsible for project management standards who was not involved in the secret meetings wrote a few comments on the model that were critical of the project management process the managers were using. The manager didn't offer any comments about the reorganization, just the way it was being done.

Unfortunately, this well-intended but not politically astute decision to participate honestly in the process was not appreciated. After being berated for a negative attitude and labeled as a non–team player, the manager was asked to remove the comment. As a bit of defiance, the manager scribbled out the comment instead of covering it over.

Not surprisingly, no one else made any other comments on the comment board. What happened? Like wildfire, everyone on the staff found out what had happened through the "grapevine" and concluded that paranoia was a rational response to this project. Management really didn't want their opinion. In the end, the passive-aggressive action by the employees worked. The reorganization was cancelled. The CIO was replaced, and the project was labeled a waste of money.

HOW TO GET PROJECTS STARTED

You learned how to start a project well in Chapter 2 ("Define") by creating visual documents of the following conversations:

- Business objectives (IRACIS)
- Scope diagram
- Project objectives
- Risks and mitigation
- Constraints
- Governance plan
- Communications plan

You also learned, in Chapter 3 ("Plan"), that by leveraging these ongoing conversations you can build a strategy for completing a quality project that is on-time and on-budget. This strategy, called the *project plan*, is expressed by a schedule with tasks that need to be done by a specific date and by specific people. Converted to a spreadsheet, this simple schedule allows you to let stakeholders know what you need from them and when, and to figure out what to do if these stakeholders aren't able to deliver.

The preceding chapters also taught you techniques to fully understand *why* your organization is doing a project so that the project plan will meet these goals. Moreover, you learned that the Define and Plan phases require a great deal of communication, including some difficult conversations. The Manage phase involves the most difficult conversations on a project. In fact, if you get the sense that managing a project is less about project management techniques and more about influencing people, then you're right.

Try this experiment. Cross your arms. No big deal, right? Now recross your arms by putting the other arm on top. How does that feel? Like something is not exactly right in your world? Well, every project creates change for the stakeholders, which makes them feel uncomfortable, even if they don't admit to it or it's right under the surface. Frankly, if no one is feeling uncomfortable about your project, then either you haven't explained it well enough or there's no reason to do the project.

The project management model that I introduced in Chapter 1 consists of these four phases:

Define answers the question *why*

Plan answers the question *how*

Manage requires seeking to *adapt*

Review requires seeking to *learn*

The model is shown again in Exhibit 4.1, along with the highlights of the Manage phase, which will be the focus of this chapter.

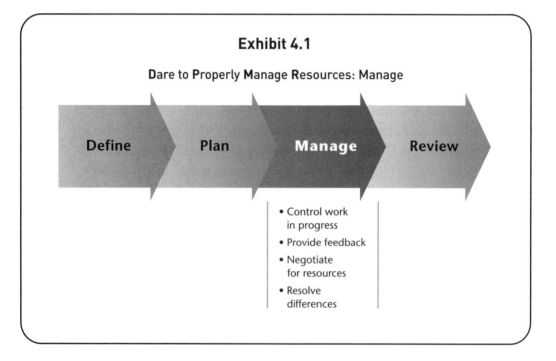

Exhibit 4.1

Dare to Properly Manage Resources: Manage

Define   Plan   **Manage**   Review

- Control work in progress
- Provide feedback
- Negotiate for resources
- Resolve differences

YOU CANNOT CONTROL A PROJECT

The Manage phase is all about *adapting*. Many of my students come in looking for techniques that will (as they usually put it) "make people do what I want them to do." If only this were possible. These students wrongly believe that good project management is all about control. If you look honestly at what interrupted your plans on your previous projects, you'll quickly see that the really bad surprises (for example, economic collapse and recession), weather, and downsizing were way beyond the scope of what you could control.

If you really believe that you have complete control over a project, then a lot of bad things are going to occur:

- You will get very angry and stressed when it turns out you can't control people
- As you get angrier, other people will get angrier with you, increasing the likelihood that they won't do what you say

Instead, you should approach your project with an attitude like this:

How can I adapt to the surprises that will come my way all through this project, and do so in a way that will maximize communication and minimize conflict?

PROJECTS TODAY

In today's work environment, the biggest challenge to your project is lack of focus. Everyone is doing more with less, juggling multiple jobs, roles, and projects. The stress of work overload on your stakeholders means you face real challenges to finish your project on time.

This chapter, on the Manage phase, explores project management techniques and strategies to help you stay focused on communication rather than control. The project charter and project plan that you create are part of a road map that helps everyone, including you, know what they are supposed to be doing. When changes have to be made, everyone will understand them.

The project plan is a critical part of Manage since this phase is directly connected to the calendar. Using the dates that you learned how to calculate in Chapter 3, you can know how ahead or behind you are on your project on a daily basis.

When change does come to your project, you are already set up to work with your project sponsor to decide what to do. You will learn more about the best ways to accomplish this work later in the chapter. The change your project will face may range from "no big deal" to devastating; it's not uncommon for the "no big deal" variety to morph into devastating change if you're not paying attention. Your investment in the Define phase really pays off here.

Here's how change may impact other key considerations of your project:

- The business objectives tend to be pretty stable. Still, keeping them part of the conversation around change ensures that you are staying true to the purpose of the project, and helps you have strategic conversations with your project sponsor.

- The scope diagram helps you determine if the change will require any additional time, money, or scope—or all of these things.

- The project objectives may change as you and the project sponsor learn what you are really up against.

- Project constraints may shift, as you'll read below. This may force you to adjust your project plan.

- You may face other unforeseen risks requiring risk mitigation activities, which you'll have to schedule on your plan.

- The communications plan may change if new stakeholders are added.

In some cases, changes may occur that make the business objective impossible to achieve, or at least unlikely. For example, a training program may no longer make sense, or a new product may have new competition. It is your responsibility as the project manager to propose to *cancel* the project. A cancelled project is not the same thing as a failed project. The best action you can take for your organization is to cancel projects that don't make sense, no matter when you figure it out. It takes great courage to cancel a project, though it takes only a few steps to cancel it in an orderly way.

The bottom line is that you must internalize the concept of *flexible structure*. You must be willing to change the plan when needed and accept the fact that your project will face challenges that have nothing to do with your talent as a project manager.

BUILDING A STATUS REPORT TO KICK OFF THE PROJECT

While it's a natural tendency to believe that once your project charter and project plan are complete it's time to rest, the hardest part is yet to come. Don't let your guard down. In Chapter 3, you solved the "puzzle" of the project schedule and created a list of tasks with owners and due dates. Now you must leverage this list to create a *project status report*.

Technique: Project Status Report

First, import your tasks into an Excel spreadsheet like the one shown in Exhibit 4.2 for our Day of Caring project. The columns should be labeled as follows:

PROJECT

> You only need this column if you are going to track multiple projects in the same spreadsheet. This will allow you to sort by project name.

TASK

> This is the description of the task you are tracking in this row.

TASK OWNER

> This is the person who is responsible for getting this task done. It is not necessarily the person or people who are doing the task, but the person you are going to hold accountable for completion. This allows you to sort by task owner if you need to.

LATEST DUE DATE

> This is the last possible date the task can be completed. It can be completed earlier, but not later, because you created this date by working back from a fixed due date. This allows you to look at the project tasks in chronological order.

COMMENTS

> This can be used for any notes you want to make about the task. I use it primarily to remember decisions that were made about changes to the task.

COMPLETED

> When a task is completed, insert a check mark (symbol) in this column. This allows you to sort all the completed tasks together.

Use Sidebar 4.1 to build your own status report spreadsheet.

Exhibit 4.2

Status Report: Day of Caring Project

Project	Task	Project Manager	Task Owner	Helpers	Due	Comments	Completed
VolDay	Establish project team	Jo	Margie	Carol	2/1/12		
VolDay	Choose charity	Jo	Carol		2/21/12	Email results	
VolDay	Invite celebrities	Jo	Margie		3/11/12	Needs approvals	
VolDay	Invite media	Jo	Beth	Margie	3/21/12		
VolDay	Arrange catering	Jo	Margie		3/21/12		

Sidebar 4.1

Your Status Report Spreadsheet

Copy the columns from the Day of Caring spreadsheet (Exhibit 4.2) to your spreadsheet. Transfer your tasks complete with task owner and due date to your spreadsheet.

After you have completed the spreadsheet and reviewed it with the project sponsor if possible, create a status report *email* to send to all the stakeholders. This is on the communications plan you created during the Define stage. You can see a sample email in Exhibit 4.3.

The email should contain the following:

- Your project schedule, cut and pasted into the bottom of the email. Do not attach the schedule, or most people won't bother to look at it. Also, everyone who does open the attachment may make changes to it in different places, creating a maintenance nightmare for you.

- An announcement about the kick-off of the project with a brief description of the value to the organization and who is sponsoring the project.

- A clear explanation that the table included in your email (your spreadsheet) shows the deliverables required for the project. You should point out that the date is the last possible delivery date for your deliverables. Encourage everyone to let you know if the due date indicated on the spreadsheet is not possible to meet, and if not, to provide this information as soon as possible.
- A status-sharing schedule (daily, weekly, monthly, and so on).
- All of your possible contact information, as part of your sign-off.

Use Sidebar 4.2 to create a model for a concise email—into which you will cut and paste your status spreadsheet—for regular distribution to your stakeholders.

Sidebar 4.2

Your Email to Stakeholders

Adapt the email sample for the Day of Caring project to language that would be more like the kind you would use. Remember to keep the email short enough to fit without scrolling down. Cut and paste the spreadsheet you just built into the email and distribute it to your stakeholders.

You are likely going to need to set up calendar reminders to make sure that you meet your own promises. In the next section, you will read about how to update and send this spreadsheet consistently to all concerned.

Potential Challenges

You may be tempted to not include some individuals in the organization such as some upper management types, but you should remember a common executive axiom: "No news is bad news." It is critical that everyone involved has an accurate idea of the status of the project, and this quick, simple approach will help you manage expectations as you begin and end the project.

As you learned when you drew the project scope diagram, it is not unusual for politics to keep you from the real project sponsor. In many cases, you must work through your immediate supervisor, and that can be a risk factor depending on how effectively your boss communicates with your sponsor. If possible, get permission from your supervisor to send this email status report to the project sponsor as a way to ensure that the expectation of the "buyer" is being managed on a consistent basis.

Strategies for Influencing Stakeholders

Choose your words carefully. Do not oversell the project. Be clear in the email about any large risks that you are worried about and how you plan to mitigate them, if it's appropriate to your internal politics.

BUILDING A PROCESS TO COMMUNICATE EARLY AND OFTEN

Once the project starts, the project manager becomes the traffic coordinator. You may also play other roles on the project, but the most important role you have is to keep all the other stakeholders moving on their tasks. Stakeholders are not necessarily familiar with the dependencies between their work and others and may not understand why their piece of the project has to be completed by the date shown on your spreadsheet. It is critical that you continue to point out the due dates to stakeholders on a regular basis, and reinforce the importance of all the pieces of the project coming together as planned.

Technique: Status Updates

Back in Chapter 2 you determined the Quick and Dirty Risk Assessment number for your project. At that time, you learned that the higher the risk number you came up with (using your instincts), the more time you would need to spend on project management. That moment has arrived.

Depending on the risk number you came up with, hold an appropriate amount of time on your calendar for uninterrupted focus on the status of your project. If yours is a really high-risk project, you might want to check the status daily. I find most times that looking at the status once a week for an hour or so is sufficient for moderate-risk projects. If the risk is really low, consider just sending updates out a few times until the project is done.

Here is what you do on your project status spreadsheet as your project progresses:

- Put a symbol such as a check mark (use Insert symbol in MS Excel) in the COMPLETED column for any task that has been completed.

- Update any comments that will improve overall communication, but keep them minimal.
- Make any other changes that are relevant (for example, has the task owner changed?).
- Mark any tasks that are late by adding a comment and changing the font color to *red* (shown as bold in Exhibit 4.4). As you'll read below ("Potential Challenges"), you should never take this step unless you've already talked to the owner about it.
- Use strikethrough type to cross out any tasks that you've decided not to do, and add a brief comment, which will keep you and others from revisiting that decision.

Sort the spreadsheet in this order:

1. COMPLETED (checkmarked rows will show up at the top and reinforce how cool you all are for getting so much done together)
2. LATEST DUE DATE (sorts rows in order of due date after the completed rows)

Exhibit 4.4 shows an example of an updated status spreadsheet, including this spreadsheet sort.

Exhibit 4.4

Weekly Status Update: Day of Caring Project

Project	Task	Project Manager	Task Owner	Helpers	Due	Comments	Completed
VolDay	Establish project team	Jo	Margie	Carol	2/1/12		✓
VolDay	**Choose charity**	**Jo**	**Carol**		**2/21/12**	**Email results**	
~~VolDay~~	~~Invite celebrities~~	~~Jo~~	~~Margie~~		~~3/11/12~~	~~Needs approvals~~	
VolDay	Invite media	Jo	Beth	Margie	3/21/12		
VolDay	Arrange catering	Jo	Margie		3/21/12		

Following the same process you used above when you sent the initial plan via email, cut and paste your updated spreadsheet into the body of your email. Compose a current-status paragraph for the start of the email, once again keeping the information to a length that will fit on a standard-size computer screen. The email should be structured like this:

- Accomplishments for the week
- Tasks that are running late and why
- Tasks that must be completed this week

Repeat this process regularly for the life of the project.

Issue Management

Many of you have spent mind-numbing hours in project status meetings listening to the same issues being brought up over and over. Someone writes each open issue down on a list, publishes that list, and brings it back to the next meeting to talk about it again. It's very frustrating because nothing gets done.

Why? For the same reasons that required you to build a project plan with task owners and a due date. Each issue brought up at a meeting should generate one or more tasks to resolve it. Each of these tasks has a task owner and a due date. Each of these tasks gets put on your spreadsheet. No need to have another list: use the one you have and communicate the issue and accountability just like you communicate every other task. Keep it moving.

Potential Challenges

Some of my students are uncomfortable marking late tasks in red. It feels confrontational to them. It's my position that there is a fine line between confronting and holding accountable. My position is that if you don't press the deadlines, you've given up the title of project manager and are responsible when the business objectives for the organization are not met.

On the other hand, if the status report is used primarily as a weapon, communication will not occur and payback behavior will increase. Walk the fine line between these two approaches: when a task is late, have a conversation with the stakeholder as soon as possible (if not on the day the task is due) to work out a strategy for completion. Explain that you are going to put the strategy in the status report. Never mark anything in red until you have discussed it, preferably face-to-face, with the stakeholder.

Strategies for Influencing Stakeholders

In 2003, D. Ford and John Stermann published a white paper titled "The Liars' Club: Concealing Rework in Concurrent Environments." Exhibit 4.5 shows a graph based on their research. In this fascinating study of 150 IT projects of different sizes, the researchers found that project managers who lied about the status of their project averaged project completion twice as long as what was planned. You'll be happy to hear that the people who told the truth about their troubles tended to come in on time and on budget. Maybe the "right prevailed" and maybe these brave project managers got the help they needed early. Of course, telling the truth may mean a political and personal risk in organizations, but the choice does seem to drive better project results.

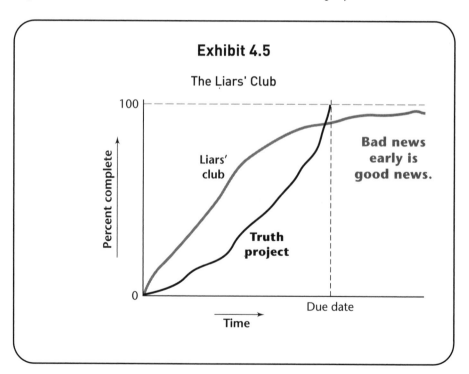

MANAGING PROJECT CHANGE

The world goes on, and change occurs all around us. We can't freeze the world. As a project progresses, expect changes to the scope, project objectives, risk, and project plan. Read that sentence again. All of those deliverables *will* change. You will learn in this section how to manage your own reactions to the changes that your stakeholders will ask for in your project. How you behave will strongly influence how others behave.

Projects always trigger change. That's the point of a project. If your project doesn't change anything, it can't be of value to your organization. Many if not all of your stakeholders may feel unsettled about the changes the project will implement. Some may feel like the changes won't have anything to do with them, and will react strongly when they find out that's not true. In this section, you'll learn ways to deal with people's unique reactions to change.

Before you continue, go to Sidebar 4.3 to think about the changes your project will bring to you and your stakeholders.

First consider the following. Do you know people at your company who are not trustworthy but with whom you have to work to get your project done? Do you consider yourself trustworthy? If I could ask those untrustworthy people the same question, how would they answer? In my classes, everyone knows someone untrustworthy, but everyone in my classes considers themselves trustworthy. Either the untrustworthy never go to training classes, or our mental models are invalid.

I believe that 99.9 percent of the time people are following the path that seems sane from their perspective. Managing change requires that you notice your assumptions and separate them from the facts you observe. Assuming ill intent is not helpful to project success, and is likely incorrect.

> ### Sidebar 4.3
> #### Reflecting on Change in Your Project
>
> Think about your project, your stakeholders, the dates, and the resources you have.
>
> What changes can you imagine this project will make on your life?
>
> What will you lose? What will you gain?
>
> What changes will impact others in the company?
>
> What will they lose and gain?
>
> How will you recognize your own emotions so that you can move through frustration and stress into possibilities?

Change and Scope

First a rule: change = scope change. Let's take a minute and review some examples of scope changes and their impact on your project charter deliverables and your project plan:

- The business objectives change. This is a *huge* change and will likely change every deliverable. For example, if you thought your project was being done to increase revenue and it turns out it is really primarily about driving cost from the business, every deliverable will likely change.

- A new stakeholder (with inputs and outputs) emerges. This will require adding the stakeholder to your scope diagram with the arrows showing the inputs and outputs. It will also add multiple new tasks to your project schedule.

- There is a new deliverable to or from an existing stakeholder. Add the flow(s), and add the new tasks to your project schedule.

- A task or group of tasks early in the project may take longer than you had planned. The natural reaction to this is to "steal" time from a future task. This *never* works; there's never extra time at the end. A better approach is to assume that this is a trend, not a fluke, and that all the estimates are off by this much. The only way to get back on schedule is to cut the scope now, by removing flows and/or stakeholders.

Rock and a Hard Place

Change usually arrives through the request of a stakeholder, perhaps one you never even knew you had! By making this change, your whole project may be impacted in some way. When you add more scope to your project, your project will need more time, more money, and likely both unless you cut out an equal amount of scope.

As a project manager, you do not own the decision to make or deny changes, but you do own the conversation. A big mistake that project managers make, especially when stressed, is to say no. It's not your place to say no. You do not own the project; the business does. Sometimes change must occur.

Instead, replace no with "Yes, and the impact will be . . ." Explain how the change will impact the completion of the project in terms of time, budget, and/or scope. Help the stakeholder understand the perspective of the business objectives and the scope of the entire project. It is likely the stakeholder is only considering his or her part of the project.

If the stakeholder believes that the change is worth the impact, determine whether the change is significant enough from your perspective. This is where your governance plan, created in Chapter 2, comes in handy. In this document, you determined how to address change requests based on the impact on time, cost, and scope. Implement this plan now. It may be that it's time to escalate this decision to your project sponsor. To escalate a decision, present the project sponsor with the change request, two to three options outlining the impact of each, as well as your recommendation. You likely have more detailed information than the project sponsor, so it is critical that you present your recommendation as part of the conversation.

When a decision is made, do what the project sponsor wants and communicate that to the stakeholder. A viable alternative might be to add the request to a list of additional requirements that will be done in the next release of the project.

The Bills Are Coming In

It's possible that you had a reasonable budget at the start of the project, but perhaps hard times forces a budget cut right in the middle of the project. Less money means you will have less (or no) help. Again, be clear with the project sponsor about the impact of this change, and cut scope with the permission of the sponsor. Sometimes a timeline is accelerated, especially if you are working on new product development projects. Once again, before cutting specific scope, you should clear it with the project sponsor.

Monsters Under the Bed

At the start of the project, it is unlikely that you'll be able to guess all the possible risks. Remember, risks are bad things that *might* happen. A risk that happens becomes a *constraint*. If something bad happens that you did not anticipate, it's still a constraint. It is possible as the project moves along that you identify a new risk down the road. For example, let's suppose that a key stakeholder is replaced and you have a fear that the new person might be a problem for your project. Take the time to listen to yourself and think through how you might mitigate the situation should this occur.

What Have We Lost? What Will We Gain?

People have fairly predictable reactions when they think their future is being threatened. Imagine that you are stretching a rubber band between your two hands, using your index fingers. One of your hands represents the way you think the world *should* be. Your other hand represents the way you see the world *is*. The farther these two hands are apart, the more tension on the rubber band. The same is true with stress, which increases as your perceived views of what *is* and what *should* be get farther apart. That's what happens during change.

Let's define some terms here. For the sake of this chapter, I'd like to differentiate between *change* and *transition*. Change is an event that occurs—in our case, some change brought to fruition through a project. It may be something that occurs that I want to have happen, but it will still feel uncomfortable at first.

Transition, on the other hand, is your choice. Notice in my description of the rubber band exercise above that both what is and what should be are our perceptions. To reduce stress, it makes sense to move either the "how I perceive things should be" hand, or the "how I see things are right now" hand. In each case, you are exercising choice.

William Bridges wrote the popular little paperback *Managing Transitions*, and his model provides a simple way to understand how people react to change, positive and negative, chosen and not. Exhibit 4.6 is a model I've created based on Bridges's work.

Notice that there are three phases—Endings, Neutral Zone, and New Beginnings—with corresponding emotional states.

Endings, the first phase, is where you find yourself when you perceive you are losing something. Let's use our project example. You are excited that you have been chosen to work on the Day of Caring project, but you are also worried that the additional workload will be more than you can handle. As it becomes evident to you that you were right about your workload concerns, you start experiencing the emotions in Endings.

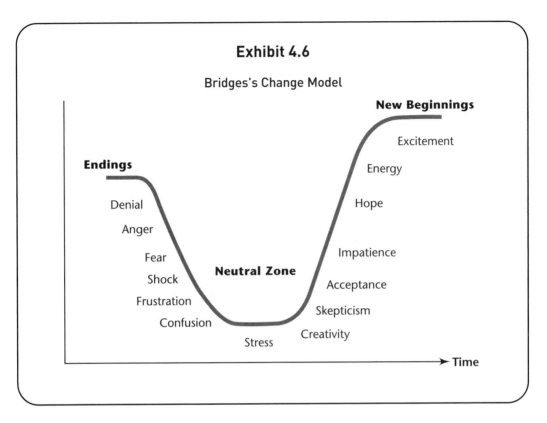

Exhibit 4.6

Bridges's Change Model

Endings

Denial

Anger

Fear

Shock

Frustration

Confusion

Stress

Neutral Zone

New Beginnings

Excitement

Energy

Hope

Impatience

Acceptance

Skepticism

Creativity

Time

In order to move through Endings, a personal admission is required that you have lost something and it's not coming back. In our example, you have to cut the scope of some of the other commitments you may have to be on the Day of Caring project. You have to say "not now" to some of your other scheduled activities, perhaps even personal ones. Until you acknowledge this Ending, internal conflict will trigger the negative emotions you see on the downward slope of the model.

Once you let go of what you've lost, you'll find yourself in the Neutral Zone. This is a state of acknowledgment that you can't recoup the past, but at the same time the future is not clear. In our example, you've made the temporary sacrifices needed, but you really don't get how, when, and why you'll be needed on the Day of Caring project. This is extremely stressful and begs the question: did you leave something good or successful for a new and doomed-to-fail project?

Moving from the Neutral Zone to New Beginnings requires a shrug of the shoulders and a different outlook. You need to say to yourself, "Oh well, I'm in it now. It's possible it will work out." Notice that the possibility you see in the New Beginnings stage doesn't have to be Nirvana-like; it just has to be something better or at least hopeful.

The emotions that surface in people during movement away from the Neutral Zone into New Beginnings can really drive a project manager crazy and can result in confrontation; for example, a frustrated project manager might say something like, "Cynicism is not a behavior I appreciate at my project meetings!" But what if we saw cynicism as a legitimate plea for help to see the future? That changes everything. Also, we might notice that impatience shortly follows cynicism. It's amazing how quickly the urge to move forward emerges after team members have plumbed the depths of the Neutral Zone.

How can you use the model to manage your stakeholders? Rather than think of negative reactions as directed toward you personally, use Bridges's model to gauge and understand your team's reactions to the phases of your project. For example, if someone is inappropriately angry, try to figure out what he thinks you are taking away from him (what is being lost). If someone is stressed to the max, then find a future of possibilities. If someone is cynical or impatient, work with her to find a reasonable metric for deliverables.

Be careful not to read the model as a flowchart; for example, if someone is angry today, they may be back in denial the next. People skip back and forth across all three phases as they move toward New Beginnings. As mentioned earlier, some people get stuck and may never leave Endings. Instead, use the model to mitigate your own negative reaction while helping others understand and move on from their own emotional states.

You may have been thinking about some of the changes that you are going through, and what your current emotional state is. Your stakeholders will have their own path through this model as your project changes their world. Use Sidebar 4.4 to think about this.

Potential Challenges

As project manager, you own the responsibility of planning, organizing, and managing your project toward a successful completion as measured by the business and project objectives. Toward the end of a successful conclusion, anything you can do to build collaboration and minimize ongoing conflict will increase common communication.

Each person owns the choice of moving toward New Beginnings or staying mired in Endings or the Neutral Zone; if the latter is the case, there may be nothing you can do. I've often thought that a dysfunctional individual could render a functional group dysfunctional, but the reverse was not true. If one of your stakeholders becomes dysfunctional, it becomes a constraint. Figure out a way to get along without these team members or at least go around them.

People do get in your way, and that's just a fact of life. It's also a fact of life that some projects are disasters. Some very large, cross-functional, multiyear, multimillion dollar projects struggle on for years and years. Other projects destroy careers or, even worse, perhaps directly affect a team member's health.

Don't let the potential insanity of projects get you down. With the right attitude and people, you'll be surprised at the creativity and resilience of most project teams.

It is much more likely that people issues will stall your project rather than project management technique issues. Conflict almost always comes from lack of communication, incorrect perception, and stress. My own instinct about team conflict tells me that when two people on a project have conflict with each other, each adds about 30 percent more time to the project.

Think about how two people feuding act. They undermine each other at every opportunity. They ask leading questions to trip each other up in meetings. They stir up drama behind the scenes and even actively work to get rid of their enemy. It's very possible that the conflict goes way back to another project or to something that has nothing to do with your project. It just shows up like an uninvited guest.

WAYS TO CREATE STRESS

Want to know the things that are guaranteed to create stress? Here are six wonderful ways to escalate tension:

- Mistrust

- Bureaucracy

- Physical separation

- Fragmentation of time

- Quality-reduced results

- Phony deadlines

Trust must be earned, but project teams must be careful not to fall into the trap of "us vs. them." Try to make sure your team learns to see the call from the client's perspective and not take the frustrated anger as an attack. Trust will eventually develop from the client side with trust from the project team side.

Bureaucracy often provides people with a safe place to be mean. Be constantly vigilant of rules that appear to your customers to be preventing good service. If your customers feel as if roadblocks are being thrown up to minimize work for your staff at their expense, their trust will disappear and they will always be on the attack. Team members need to have the autonomy to solve the problems they are supposed to solve and say no when they are being asked to do something outside their charter. This requires lots of discussion and communication, and it never ends.

Many team members never get to see the faces of the people they serve. Figure out some creative ways to reduce the physical separation, which only feeds "us vs. them." Make site visits, have open houses, and do lots of things to make the project team personal. It's a little tougher to be mean to someone you know. This will ultimately reduce the stress for everyone.

In a multitiered environment, many lower-tier team members get all the flack and none of the glory. Their job is to take the call, weather the storm, and pass the problem on if it requires more than a knowledge-base access. This may be efficient, but it is very damaging to the front line because there is no reinforcement that their work has any importance. Consider creating a process that lets lower-tier team members call customers back to get their feedback on whether the problem has been solved, and how. Not only will this reinforce their value, it will also increase their knowledge of the customer.

Many teams, when faced with impossible workloads, choose to have phony deadlines and end up compromising the quality of their project. In an attempt to meet all needs, they meet none. This creates nothing but hate and discontent. A more beneficial method is to reduce the scope to ensure that project needs are being met.

Use Sidebar 4.5 to examine how you may be accidentally increasing stress in others.

CONFLICT AND PROJECT SUCCESS

Conflict is a necessary component of teamwork. You shouldn't necessarily think of it as negative. Conflict handled well creates many benefits for an organization. Well-managed conflict:

- Leads to corrective action
- Diffuses future bigger conflict
- Helps organizations prioritize
- Promotes learning
- Builds cohesiveness

Make a regular habit of sharing conflict situations during team meetings. This allows team members to vent (you might even bring in a stuffed animal as a frustration punching bag) without taking it out on the client, and it also allows you the breathing room to step back and say, "What can we learn from this?" Often conflict comes from misunderstood facts or misplaced feelings from things like ambiguous boundaries, differing interests, value differences, communication barriers, or unresolved prior conflict.

As project manager, you are responsible for making sure everything assigned to the stakeholders on the project scope diagram gets done. You own all the flows and all the project tasks. If conflict occurs on your project and it impedes the progress of any tasks, you are responsible for getting it resolved. Here's how:

First, speak to those in conflict individually. Avoid starting your sentences with the word *you*. Instead, start by saying something like, "I have noticed that you and Jo have some conflict, and I'd like to know how you two can resolve it so it no longer stalls this project." If necessary, bring the two people together in your presence or the presence of a facilitator from your HR function to referee the conversation. If these steps are not effective, escalate the problem to your project sponsor with suggestions for who would be better as replacements.

Technique: Moment of Awareness

Moment of Awareness (MA) is the practice of noticing what is happening to you right now. You can teach yourself to notice when stress is starting and step outside of yourself for a moment to analyze it logically and then react. Here's a list of thoughts and entrenched ideas that can easily cause problems:

- I am my position
- The enemy is out there
- Try harder, faster, take charge, push
- Fixate on events and blame

The truth is:

- Today's problems are from yesterday's solutions
- The harder you push, the harder you get pushed back
- Behavior gets worse before it gets better
- The easy way out leads back in
- The cure can be worse than the disease
- Faster is slower
- Cause and effect are not always closely related in time

CREATING PERSONAL RESILIENCY

As a project manager, you live in an environment of constant change. Depending on your behavioral strength, your previous project experiences, your emotional competence, your overall health, and how much sleep you've been getting, your stress could physiologically impact your decision-making ability. In this section, you will:

- Define resiliency and learn the practices
- Identify your emotional awareness and ability to regulate your emotions
- Leverage your behavioral strengths to regulate your emotions and create the focus you need for difficult project decisions
- Learn Spiral Impact techniques to regain composure when you have experienced a strongly negative emotion
- Learn to let people leave with the monkeys they came in with

One night, years ago, my husband and I arrived at Myrtle Beach at the height of the summer crowds. It was the middle of the night, and we had three small children in tow. We were all cranky. As the veteran traveler, I had made the reservations. I marched in to get the key to our condo for the week. The front desk person informed me that the facility was overbooked, and we wouldn't get the room until the next afternoon. When the manager helped us discover that every hotel in the area was booked, I chose to go ballistic and threaten him with everything I could think of before storming out to the car in tears to scream at my husband.

My husband offered to go talk to the manager, which made me even madder. My older daughter decided to go along with my husband, just to get away from me, I'm sure. After about ten minutes, my daughter came back to tell me that she thought Dad had gotten a room for us. I demanded to know what her father had done to get a room. My daughter said that my husband had volunteered to help clean up our room (apparently our condo was available, but not serviced). And so we got a room.

You can see what happened. As soon as I lost my temper, my options became more limited. I lost the ability to think of a creative solution. The angry but innocent desk clerk had no reason to help me. My husband saved the day, because he chose to use smiles and dumb jokes to work with the tired clerk to meet both our needs. That's what resiliency is about.

You'll enjoy the activity in Sidebar 4.6 alone, but you'll learn more if you instruct a group of your friends through it and watch what they do. The sidebar leads you through the steps. Be aware of your emotional energy as you do each step.

Sidebar 4.6

Resiliency and You

Find a piece of paper and fold it twice into four quadrants. In each quadrant you are going to quickly sketch a picture following my instructions, taking less than 30 seconds for each one.

- First: Draw a sketch of a house.
- Second: With your other hand, draw a sketch of a flower.
- Third: Go back to using your dominant hand. Draw a sketch of a cat with your eyes closed.
- Fourth: Switch to your other hand one more time. Draw a sketch of a tree with this hand *and* your eyes closed.

To really appreciate this exercise, gather some people together at lunch and walk them through the same steps. Watch how they behave as you move from a very simple project to an almost impossible one. What happens?

It's likely that you and your fellow participants drew seriously in the first quadrant, silently and with little sharing. Your goal was to check it off, get it done. Drawing with the other hand in the second quadrant was a bit more difficult and the resulting drawing not so good. The drawing in the third quadrant, with your eyes closed, likely caused your group to laugh hysterically with each other. After quadrant four, most people look at everyone else's pictures first, and say complimentary things about their own like, "It's really not that bad!"

It makes no sense. Why do people have more fun when the project is harder, or actually ludicrous? But why not? If the project is ridiculous, anything you get done is amazing. What if you carried this with you to your project? How would it feel if everything you accomplished was viewed with amazement especially because the time and budget were so limited?

We get to decide whether we see our projects as opportunities to do amazing things or opportunities to fall on our face. As project manager, keep your eyes on the possibilities of your projects and avoid drowning in the constant little challenges. The ability to think creatively requires this outlook. If you think your project is impossible, you are right. The opposite is also true. Fear will paralyze you.

Stop Looking Through Dirty Water

"Emotional intelligence" is an important part of managing a project. Daniel Goleman coined the term EQ (a play on the acronym IQ) in his important book by the same name. Here's an illustration of how emotions influence project management. Imagine the difference between looking across the room through a glass of muddy water and a glass of clear water. The muddy water represents how our decision making is impacted by negative emotions. Our minds were designed to keep us safe. Every moment your brain is scanning around you to see what might threaten you. Luckily, most of us are not physically threatened very often, but our brain also picks up threats to our self-esteem.

The brain reacts to these threats by immediately moving into survival mode. In the learning field, we refer to this as a reptilian-brain response, the most primitive of our brain functions. It is an automatic response, so don't even try to stop it from emerging. Through hormonal intervention, the heart rate accelerates and blood is sent to the arms and legs so you are all set to punch or run as the need arises.

To focus on survival, the brain shuts down some of the frontal lobe where decision-making competence is located. Long-term memory is also shut down a bit, further degrading your ability to make a decision other than to run or fight back. In our current workplaces, this would be translated into hide/leave or yell/get angry.

There is some evidence that our brains were designed for one or two big threats a day, like a lion-sighting on the African plains. In our work lives, it is more likely that we will feel dozens of personal attacks during the day. Although these attacks are not as alarming, they exhaust the brain because it does not get the rest it needs to gear up for the next attack. Thanks to email, we get a constant stream of these attacks.

Izzy Justice's research in his book *Emotional Quotient* shows that after a significantly strong emotional threat, the brain has a four-hour "emotional hangover." For up to four hours you will be unable to make a good project decision.

I like to think of the reptilian-brain response as a rusty gate that's closing. At the beginning, the gate swings very slowly and can still be stopped from slamming shut. After a certain point of no return, the gate gains speed and slams completely shut, and the four-hour hangover begins. The trick is learning how to recognize that the gate has begun to close and mitigate the situation before the gate shuts completely.

A little stress is a good thing for creativity. The concept of cognitive dissonance is something we leverage in training design frequently. Leaving learners hungry for a little something motivates them to learn it. In projects, cognitive dissonance can be leveraged to help us become resilient and creatively come up with alternative plans. Exhibit 4.7 shows how our productivity flows from our "emotional intelligence," or EQ, tend to invest a lot in helping people

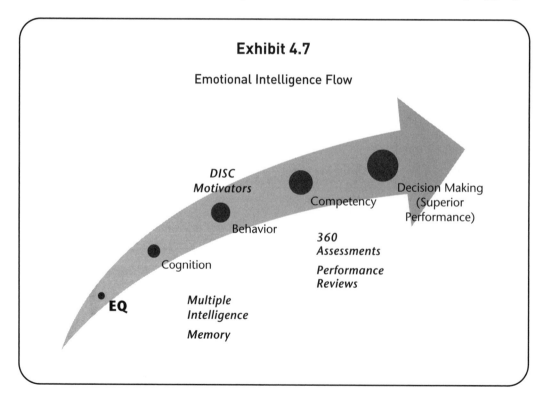

Exhibit 4.7

Emotional Intelligence Flow

DISC
Motivators

Behavior

Competency

Decision Making
(Superior
Performance)

Cognition

*360
Assessments*

*Performance
Reviews*

EQ

*Multiple
Intelligence*

Memory

grow awareness of their behavioral strengths (for example, DISC profiles). We train them in new competencies. And yet when people are stressed to the max, it knocks out all the great "building" that we have done.

Technique: Behavioral Profiles

To influence others, you must first know yourself. You have preferences for being influenced, and you try to use those on others. But everyone is different. Using behavioral profiles, you can identify your own behavioral strengths and weaknesses, and then use this knowledge to identify and temporarily adapt to people whom you'd like to connect with. I recommend using DISC profiles (a simplified overview of the model is in Exhibit 4.8) as a simple, quick way to identify these differences and ways to adapt. The DISC profile is also useful

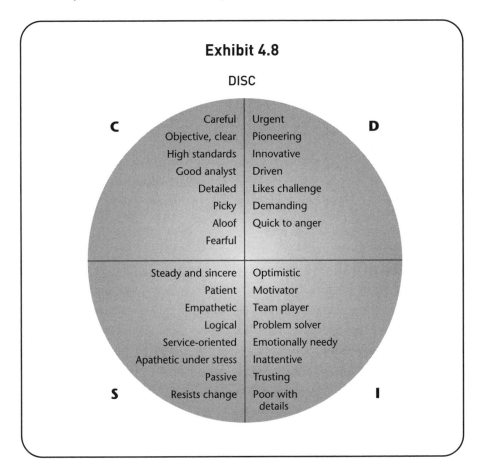

Exhibit 4.8

DISC

C		D
Careful	Urgent	
Objective, clear	Pioneering	
High standards	Innovative	
Good analyst	Driven	
Detailed	Likes challenge	
Picky	Demanding	
Aloof	Quick to anger	
Fearful		

S		I
Steady and sincere	Optimistic	
Patient	Motivator	
Empathetic	Team player	
Logical	Problem solver	
Service-oriented	Emotionally needy	
Apathetic under stress	Inattentive	
Passive	Trusting	
Resists change	Poor with details	

to identify ways to regulate your emotions that will work for your particular style. In fact, Justice has teamed with TTI International to create an EQ/DISC combination assessment for this purpose. Contact us at www.russellmartin.com for more information.

Take a minute and think about times when your emotions may have had the best of you. Use Sidebar 4.7 to grow your own awareness of the kinds of things that shut you down during projects.

If you are like 90 percent of my students, you probably wrote *frustration* or *stress*. If your emotional gate is completely closed, you may have written stronger words like *rage*. One of my creative groups wrote *franxious*, a combination of *frustrated* and *anxious*. By understanding what triggers these types of emotional reactions, you can grow your emotional awareness and learn ways to regulate your natural emotions.

EQ assessments are also useful for learning about your emotional awareness and regulation. Emotional competence is not fixed at birth, and is something that you can grow with practice. Think of emotional maturity as leveraging three steps (see below), but always being able to improve each step in parallel as you experience change.

> **Sidebar 4.7**
>
> **Becoming Aware of Negative Emotions**
>
> Think of a project you were on recently, and write down a negative emotion you experienced. Rate that emotion from 1 to 10, 10 being the most extreme. Now write down three things that triggered that emotion. Next, try to remember how this emotion may have influenced your behavior. Did you shut down? Write down your thoughts. Repeat the exercise for other instances you can recall.

Emotional Maturity

The *first step* is self-awareness. This is your ability to notice your emotions as they occur and identify the real reason they are happening. Howard Gardner wrote about this "intelligence" in a more recent book titled *Intelligence Reframed: Multiple Intelligences for the 21st Century,* which expanded his original seven Multiple Intelligences to ten. In projects, this intelligence, or competence, is extremely important because of our need to be able to make immediate great decisions under very stressful conditions.

Izzy Justice, mentioned earlier, recommends that you pick a stressful time of day (many people say 3PM in the workday) and set an alarm for that time (you might use your cell phone). When the alarm goes off, quickly make a note of your emotional state and the severity of your current state using a number from 1 to 10. After a week or so of charting your emotional state, you should have a good picture of how your emotions are interfering with your ability to be the amazing person you really are. Assessments are also powerful ways to look at your emotional awareness. If you are in the middle of a project, you might do this exercise every time you leave a project meeting.

With an awareness of the intensity of your negative emotional reactions, you can move to the *second step* of the process—regulation and discovery of what triggers these emotions. Ask yourself, "What happened that started the reptilian-brain response?" and "What in me was threatened by that trigger?" With that information you can find an answer to the most important question: "How can I regulate this negative emotion?"

It's important to note here that the solution is not to avoid negative triggers or pretend that you are not experiencing a reptilian-brain response with a big, fake smile. This is clearly not healthy or helpful. Instead, imagine debriefing yourself on the event as you probe the root causes of your emotional reaction.

Justice's research shows that we have 80 emotional experiences a year on average that we can learn from. Justice also says that most people learn or adapt from only three events. It won't take much effort to improve that number for a project manager! Notice the emotion; notice the trigger. Then challenge the validity of the assumptions that sent you down the trail to emotional shutdown.

Finally, in the *third step*, once you've made a little progress with your own awareness and regulation, you are ready as a project manager (aka leader) to help others. Show other team members how to start their journey so they can improve their project management decision making. You can't do this journey for others, but you can coach them by giving them the support they need, if they are willing.

Technique: Pause and Grow

Karen Valencic (www.spiralimpact.com), a subject-matter expert in conflict resolution, teaches that staying calm and balanced is at the core of performance. Here Karen shares some personal insights:

I learned quickly and hard: technical expertise and organizational skills alone don't make for successful project management. Success was largely determined by my ability to influence and build relationships. As a degreed engineer, this was particularly tricky as I didn't learn "relationship" in school. Influencing people who don't report to you is an art all unto itself. This is particularly true when the people on whom you are depending have no direct commitment to your project.

For a young woman engineer in the early '80s this was intimidating. How was I to gain respect, get the job done, and not be in constant battle? It was clear to me that my "emotional" intelligence, my ability to not take things so personally and keep my cool when things got hot, was the key to excelling in my profession. But, how?

I've heard the phrase, when the student is ready the teacher appears. That was certainly true for me. My teacher continues to be the martial art, aikido. Aikido vividly teaches that influence and power come from position, not force. When dealing with an obstacle, you move with it in a spiral motion rather than head on against it. This dramatically increases your ability to influence your opponent. This concept is so simple, yet not easy. It requires self-discipline particularly on an emotional level.

Spiral Impact® is a phrase I coined to describe this method. At its core, literally, is a concept I refer to as "centering." "Centering" is becoming the calm eye of the storm. You likely have already experienced the feeling of "center." Recall a time you felt anything was possible; your senses were heightened, and time disappeared. Often, this is experienced when engaged in a stimulating project, in nature, meditation, athletics, or in relationships. This is a state of being you can recreate at your choosing.

When "centered" you witness your emotions without being a slave to them, i.e., you can notice you are angry or fearful but you don't act on your emotions. So, those times when you'd just like to do it all yourself and avoid dealing with those difficult people whose priorities are different—centering gives you the courage to make a different choice—spiral in and make a positive impact.

So how can you bring "center" to work and increase your emotional intelligence? At the end of the day, it's simply an investment of your attention and time. As I said earlier, it is simple, not easy. Can you commit to a discipline of breathing and visualizing daily? No money or extra time is required, just your focus. The ROI is off the chart!

Potential Challenges

In 1999, the *Harvard Business Review* article titled "Management Time: Who's Got the Monkey?" by William Oncken Jr., Donald L. Wass, and Stephen R. Covey became an instant hit. The premise in the article is that most people who work for, with, or around you come to you with monkeys on their back, and have the goal of leaving the monkeys with you. A good leader knows how to help others see the monkeys on their backs *and* keep them when they leave. As a project manager, watch out for other people's monkeys.

Strategies for Influencing Stakeholders

In the *Fifth Discipline Fieldbook*, you will find a great tool called the Ladder of Inference (see Exhibit 4.9 for one of my interpretations of this technique). As the pressures of a project increase, project managers must work hard to separate the facts from the add-ons and interpretations. As you can see in

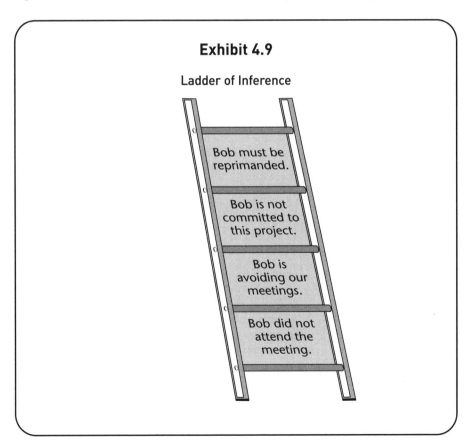

Exhibit 4.9

Ladder of Inference

Bob must be reprimanded.

Bob is not committed to this project.

Bob is avoiding our meetings.

Bob did not attend the meeting.

this example, a simple fact like Bob not attending a meeting is interpreted as Bob's lack of commitment to the project, and that false assumption leads to confrontation. From the outside looking in, most of us can see that this is not going to bring a productive end to the project status meeting. But from the inside, it is very easy to forget what is triggering negative emotions—false assumptions.

Search for and embrace facts. Discourage discussions of interpretations of self and others.

 Lou's Project Management Diary

While teaching project management at an oil company years ago, I was approached by a student after class who asked for help communicating with his boss. He felt that every time he sent a status report to the boss, the response was increasingly negative. He had decided that the boss's negative response to him was due to the fact that he hadn't spent enough time making the basic email status reports pretty. So he intended to spend that evening really making a sensational status report with colors, fonts, and everything that would make it look like it was created for a television audience.

I asked the student to describe the behavior of his boss—how he liked to work, what conversations were like with him, when he was more engaged. I asked him to describe a time when he and his boss had really connected. After listening to these stories, I suggested an experiment before he pulled an all-nighter creating a multimedia presentation. I told him to stick his head in his boss's office door on his way out and give him a 30-second update on the project with no fluff, details, or questions.

As a consultant, you never know what's going to happen when you suggest something like this, so I nervously waited to hear the news the next day. The student came in beaming and reported that his boss was the kind of person who wanted the facts, concise and fast. This was the best way to communicate with him.

It is critical when influencing others during a project to remember that everyone is different. Most important, everyone does not like the same things you like. Know yourself, and learn how to identify the preferences of others so that you can adapt your communication on the fly with the people you need to get the project done.

SUMMARY CHECKLIST

In this chapter you learned how to:

- Build a quick, Excel-based status report to email to stakeholders

- Leverage this status report by updating it with predictable frequency and honesty

- Be aware that lying about the project guarantees you will receive bad news *late*

- Apply resiliency practices to turn impossible projects into different projects

- Identify your emotional awareness and ability to regulate your emotions

- Leverage your behavioral strengths to regulate your emotions and create the focus you need for difficult project decisions

- Apply Spiral Impact techniques to regain composure when you have experienced a strongly negative emotion

- Help people leave with the monkeys they came in with

CHAPTER 5

Review

"Each participant in a project is sane from his perspective, but together we often create insanity."

In this chapter:

- Four ways (emotion-based, standard survey, learning histories, causal loop diagrams) to facilitate postproject reviews

- How to leverage the knowledge gained from the review for the growth of your personal competence

- How to create a process to share project-management lessons learned to jump-start new projects

- How to create a peer mentoring program to leverage and grow project-management shared knowledge through social learning

Lou's Project Management Diary

Conseco, a large insurance company, requested a detailed post-project review after struggling for multiple years to implement a large, cross-functional software project. Individuals representing all the stakeholder groups were invited to participate in a two-day facilitation (rare to have this much time today!) to figure out what went wrong and how to avoid the same pitfalls going forward. At the start of the session, the attendees were clustered with the others from their factions and braced for more corporate war. The body language of crossed arms, "dare me" facial expressions, and lots of side-talk smirks was daunting to me as a facilitator.

I decided to use Systems Thinking to create a model that would accomplish two things: show clearly what had happened to help and hinder project progress; and keep things "blameless." We started by creating the Nirvana loop, showing how the project would have progressed if everything had gone perfectly. Then each area modeled the story from their perspective, telling the story of why Nirvana didn't happen, at least not all the time.

Similar to the gears of an old-fashioned pocket watch, the combined model communicated to everyone that all the individual stories influenced each other with sometimes surprisingly destructive results. One eye-opening example was the role of the project manager. Every time something fell apart on the project, the company would replace the current project manager with a project manager from a successful project. The net effect was that both projects floundered. Adding people to a struggling project rarely works, especially at the top.

In Chapters 2–4, you learned how to: start a project well by creating visual documents of critical, difficult assumptions; build a schedule honoring these assumptions; then manage these documents while knowing full well that the world is changing constantly, and that so too will your project. Approaching a project thinking about "managing" instead of "controlling" gives you the power to be agile in times of chaos. And believe me, chaos reigns. If you don't see it, then you're not really paying attention.

In this chapter, you'll learn how to take a very short breather from too much work in order to learn from a completed project. Chances are, you are currently juggling multiple projects, and the completion of one project just launches you into another. But if you take a little time to reflect on what went well and what you would have done differently, your project management competence will continue to improve.

As you remember, the project management model introduced in the first chapter consists of these four phases:

Define answers the question *why*

Plan answers the question *how*

Manage requires seeking to *adapt*

Review requires seeking to *learn*

Once again, you'll see the model in Exhibit 5.1, with the highlights of the Review phase.

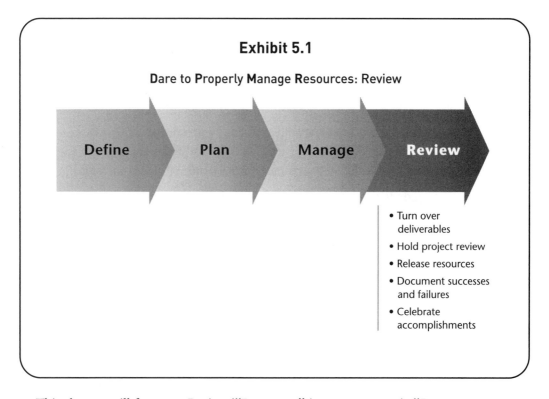

Exhibit 5.1

Dare to Properly Manage Resources: Review

Define   Plan   Manage   **Review**

- Turn over deliverables
- Hold project review
- Release resources
- Document successes and failures
- Celebrate accomplishments

This chapter will focus on *Review* ("Resources" in our mnemonic "Dare to Properly Manage Resources").

REVIEWING A COMPLETED PROJECT

The Review phase is used to take a big-picture look at the project, quickly answering the question from multiple angles:

What can I learn from this project that will help me be more effective at my future project work?

Review simply gives you the space to stand back a bit from the day-to-day chaos of a project to look from beginning to end at the choices you made that either influenced the success of the project or added to the chaos and rework. Review can take a full day or a few minutes, depending on your personal situation. It is very rarely done, which explains why project management as practiced in the real world doesn't seem to get much better, and why there is very little "new" material about project management.

How you approach projects from the start predicts whether you'll be open to thinking about how they went. If you approach projects thinking you will control them, you may avoid doing a review because of your feelings of failure. If you approach projects thinking that insanity will happen that must be managed, you will be more likely to take a minute to learn and internalize.

The larger the project and the more cross-functional it is, the more important it is to do a review. Such projects are also more difficult because the value comes from sharing the perspectives of all the diverse stakeholders. The most powerful reviews I have been part of have come from these larger projects. Some of the lessons learned included simple actionable ideas such as:

- The tendency for management to bring in a new and successful project management team from elsewhere to save a project in trouble. As stated at the start of the chapter, this paralyzes both the old and new teams.

- The fact that meetings can be either a huge waste of time or the best thing to keep a project on track. Meeting management is critical to project success.

- If project management techniques are skipped and documentation (especially around the project scope and project schedule) is not kept up-to-date and easily accessible, everyone on the project will need access to the project manager to understand their tasks and role. This will overwhelm the project manager and minimize the attention paid to keeping the documentation up-to-date—a vicious cycle.

- Adding new technology or processes to a complex project will paralyze it. When doing a large project, avoid the temptation to add process improvement components "while you're in there." Instead, work on reducing complexity.

- Leadership means delegation. Delegate, delegate, delegate—and then hold everyone accountable.

I have discovered both in my work and in my classes that everyone is managing numerous smaller projects. If this observation describes you, then consider blocking time on your calendar quarterly to look at all your projects and review what you have learned. There will be projects on your list that are low risk and just seem to get done; there will also be projects you've never done before that trigger lots of lessons learned.

Here are three things to think about when doing a postproject review:

1. How long should I wait after completion?
2. Who should be involved?
3. How can I create a blame-free analysis of the project?

How Long Should I Wait?

If you do the review a few days or weeks after a project ends, you may still be too emotionally drained to be able to take a neutral look at it. On the other hand, with today's workloads, if you wait more than a couple of months after the project, you'll likely have a lot of trouble getting anyone to help you, and you'll probably end up not doing the review. Here are some guidelines:

- If the project has more than five or six major stakeholders, schedule a two-hour project review session in the original project plan after the completion date. The date may have to be adjusted, but manage the expectation that there will be a review and that it's not optional.

- If the project has fewer than five major stakeholders, consider using a web survey or email to get feedback a month or so after you finish up the deliverables. Follow up with the stakeholders to make sure they take five minutes to give you feedback.

- If the project turned into a major disaster for your company before it was "saved," invest in a one-day workshop with a trained facilitator to get to the heart of the problems that blew up the project. It's best to wait at least two months after the project cuts before doing this, but schedule it as early as possible to ensure participation. Getting a commitment from the project sponsor to attend will help attendance as well. If you can have the invitation come from the project sponsor, it's a big help.

Who Should Be Involved?

Each of your stakeholders on your scope diagram will be represented by people on your project plan. Multiple people may be involved in the project, but you likely don't need all of them at the meeting. The discussion is best with a diversity of perspectives and fewer than ten participants so that everyone has ample time to participate. I've done reviews for groups as large as 20 and 30 people and had to break them into subgroups to manage the communication. Be sure to include the following elements:

- If personal or functional conflict occurred during the project, make sure you have representatives from all parties of the conflict

- Include anyone who was involved in testing and receiving the final deliverable (training, software, and so on)

- Include anyone who was involved in defining the initial requirements

- Include technical experts who were key to designing and implementing the deliverables

- Include a few "users" of the final deliverables

How Can I Create a Blame-Free Analysis?

Asking this question is critical if you want to get good information, but more important, getting answers to this question is critical to the success of future projects. If your review session continues to ratchet up the conflict, you can expect the same dynamic to show up during the next project if the same individuals are working on the project. In the techniques that follow I've included some processes for helping people tell their story in a safe way.

Please note that the facilitator must enforce the rules consistently and fairly. I have a yellow football penalty flag that I use for this purpose. If someone makes a comment that encourages personal conflict, I throw the penalty flag near that person and call a penalty. Then I ask the individual to repeat what she said in a way that focuses on the incident and not the individual. Finally, I leave the penalty flag with the individual who made the comment and assign him the responsibility of catching the next infraction of the rules. It's a great technique that keeps the conversation nonthreatening while encouraging accountability.

Prerequisites to the Meeting

When discussing the completed project, it is easy for those involved to try to expand the scope. If you are putting in a new training program, participants will have all kinds of suggestions for what else should go in it. If you are putting in a new technology system, there are always lots of ways the programs can be enhanced or changed. This is not what a review is about. The review is about the process of project management, and how it can be improved in the future. For that reason, make sure you have a copy of the scope diagram and business and project objectives to ensure that everyone is on the same page as far as what the goals were. Brainstorming new requirements for future releases will be another meeting.

In the next sections, you will learn four ways to do a project review. We will move from those taking the least amount of time to the most.

EMOTION-BASED REVIEW

This is my favorite way to do a quick review. You can use this technique through web surveys or in a quick face-to-face meeting (30 minutes to an hour). Thinking about our emotions helps identify very detailed memories. This survey leverages the strong memories associated with strong emotions to get at the most important things that happened to an individual during the project, both good and bad. Exhibit 5.2 shows the survey questions.

The order of the questions is critical. Begin by asking people to put a name on the emotion. Asking them to rank the emotion's intensity forces them to get more deeply into their memory, and think more about the details. This facilitates a list of triggers that really mattered to them at the time. Had you asked them from the start to identify the emotional triggers, it would have been more difficult to do this work (and likely less important to them).

Exhibit 5.2

Emotion-Based Survey Items

1. Describe the problems experienced on the project by entering on this line the emotion you felt: _____

2. What factors contributed to your feelings about the problems?

3. Describe the successes experienced on the project by entering on this line the emotion you felt: _____
Rank the intensity of that emotion (1 = low, 10 = high): _____

4. What factors contributed to your feelings about the successes?

You may notice with this technique that you get very similar answers to the first questions about negative emotions. It is very common for participants to offer *frustration* or *stress* as answers. There will also be consistency around the triggers. Many triggers have to do with holding people accountable, lack of management support, and inadequate communication. You may also find more diversity in the emotions and triggers you get from the positive side. People tend to be motivated in very unique ways.

Potential Challenges

This approach can get to the problems and successes of a project pretty quickly, but it does not generate discussion around how to change the way things were done to avoid the bad and leverage the good. You may need to have additional conversations and problem solving to translate the problems and benefits into a list of ways to improve.

STANDARD SURVEY

This is a very traditional way to do a review survey. Unlike the Emotion-Based Review, this approach creates a list of possible problem areas. You can conduct this review through a web survey (5–15 minutes).

This technique helps to remind team members of areas of project management they might not have considered. Exhibit 5.3 shows the survey questions.

Potential Challenges

This survey "leads the witness" a bit. A human tendency is to criticize when asked for feedback. For example, if you asked one of your stakeholders to rank the usefulness of the project schedule, it's pretty likely that they would tell you they needed more time, but that might not be completely accurate; it might be more a reflexive criticism.

No prioritization exists in this survey approach unless you put in a question that asks the respondent to rank the questions. Similarly, this approach does not generate discussion around how to change the way things were done during the project to avoid the bad and leverage the good. Again, you may need to have additional conversations and problem solving to translate the problems and benefits into a list of ways to improve future projects.

LEARNING HISTORIES

This approach can be done through a web survey or online discussion group, but because of the intensity of the experience, I prefer to use this technique face-to-face. Prior to the session, each participant will take approximately 30 minutes to create a Learning History. The combined session can be done in 60–90 minutes with a strong facilitator.

This approach leverages storytelling to get to the successes and challenges of a project. By asking people to remember something that happened that was typical for the project, you are letting people share their unique perspective during the project. It is always surprising to hear what someone else saw or heard, when you had assumed something entirely different. This technique helps illustrate that we are all sane from our perspective on a project but that

Exhibit 5.3

Standard Survey Items

1. Planned schedule *Comments:*	1 2 3 4 5 6 7 8 9 10 Lowest Highest	Not Applicable
2. Actual time used *Comments:*	1 2 3 4 5 6 7 8 9 10 Lowest Highest	Not Applicable
3. Planned budget *Comments:*	1 2 3 4 5 6 7 8 9 10 Lowest Highest	Not Applicable
4. Actual budget used *Comments:*	1 2 3 4 5 6 7 8 9 10 Lowest Highest	Not Applicable
5. Requirements clearly defined *Comments:*	1 2 3 4 5 6 7 8 9 10 Lowest Highest	Not Applicable
6. Project staffing and roles *Comments:*	1 2 3 4 5 6 7 8 9 10 Lowest Highest	Not Applicable
7. Project communication *Comments:*	1 2 3 4 5 6 7 8 9 10 Lowest Highest	Not Applicable
8. Implemented technology *Comments:*	1 2 3 4 5 6 7 8 9 10 Lowest Highest	Not Applicable
9. Monitoring of project progress *Comments:*	1 2 3 4 5 6 7 8 9 10 Lowest Highest	Not Applicable
10. Tools and techniques used *Comments:*	1 2 3 4 5 6 7 8 9 10 Lowest Highest	Not Applicable
11. Research and development when needed *Comments:*	1 2 3 4 5 6 7 8 9 10 Lowest Highest	Not Applicable
12. Vendor involvement *Comments:*	1 2 3 4 5 6 7 8 9 10 Lowest Highest	Not Applicable
13. Internal service organization involvement *Comments:*	1 2 3 4 5 6 7 8 9 10 Lowest Highest	Not Applicable

© Russell Martin and Associates; www.russellmartin.com

sometimes those perspectives combine to create insanity. Exhibit 5.4 shows the prerequisite assignment.

Exhibit 5.4

Preparing a Learning History

You are going to be attending a meeting to capture lessons learned about the project we just created. Please prepare for the meeting by doing the following:

1. Think of an example of a situation that impeded the progress of the project.

2. On a separate piece of paper, tell the story of what happened in a few paragraphs.

3. Bring this story to the meeting. You will be sharing it with the rest of the team.

Participants are expected to attend the meeting with their stories written. I have asked participants to bring a printed copy, but if you'd rather be a bit more green, create a shared folder on a server or use any common social networking site so that participants can read along on their laptops. The process goes like this:

- Each person reads his or her story while others read along and make notes. This proceeds, without questions, until all participants have shared their stories.

- The facilitator leads a discussion to capture "Lessons Learned"—what can we do differently and what project elements should remain the same based on the stories heard?

- The group prioritizes the Lessons Learned.

You will be surprised how powerful this technique is. Typing up their story and then reading it seems to give people the courage to share the story exactly, and not minimize or gloss over things that might be difficult. By keeping people from asking questions until everyone has gone, and then restricting these questions to Lessons Learned, you have established a safe way to look at very difficult times.

Potential Challenges

This exercise can be pretty scary to some people, and you may have some no-shows who you really don't want to lose in the discussion. If you think that's going to happen, ask everyone to bring their laptops and have them write their stories at the start of the meeting using the same criteria.

CAUSAL LOOP DIAGRAMS (SYSTEMS THINKING)

Systems Thinking is a powerful technique that allows teams to define the entire problem blamelessly so that a thorough solution plan can be implemented. It creates a visual model of different people's perspectives. Each story is combined to create a cause-and-effect model that reflects what happened but also shows what to do to improve the entire system. This is also the most time-consuming review, and is probably best done on large, multifunctional projects. It works best if you set aside one day for model building and then another day, preferably a few days later, for action planning. You will need a facilitator trained in this type of facilitation to ensure success.

Every individual's view of the problem is sane, given his or her data. Yet when combined, those sane views can create insanity. It isn't anyone's fault; it is the fault of the complex and often-accidental system. In this case the word *system* means the variables and influences on a project taken together. Simple questions such as, "Why are our projects failing to meet their budget and time goals?" usually cannot be answered with simple responses. Therefore, the solution must be complex and systemic if it is to have an impact and address all parts of the whole. Quick fixes often fail because they focus on just one part of the problem rather than the problem as a whole.

Peter Senge's *The Fifth Discipline* states that the key to business success is for organizations to become learning organizations that learn from both successes and failures. Systems Thinking is a technique for analyzing and modeling the causes and effects of complex problems, and then separating these elements into manageable pieces so they are better understood before solutions are designed. Systems Thinking is best used on the types of issues that keep reappearing despite everyone's best efforts. These issues include:

- Why are our project skills lacking?
- Why is project management training ineffective?
- Why is it difficult to get IT to collaborate with its internal customers?

The best way to see how Systems Thinking can help you learn more about a problem is to look at an example. Exhibit 5.5 is a Systems Thinking model answering, in part, the question, "Why do projects fail?" It looks overwhelming, but each loop represents one story (or one perspective). This model is called a Causal Loop Diagram. It reflects the story of the specific group of people involved in creating it, so for that reason it may not necessarily represent your story. It is their perceived truth, which is the reality they worked within.

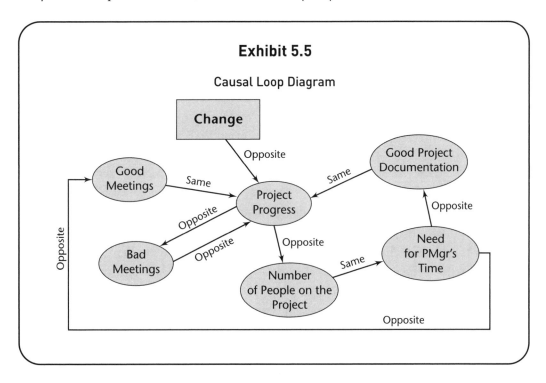

Exhibit 5.5

Causal Loop Diagram

To read this model, review the center loop, starting with the variable "Project Progress." As you can see, there are multiple arrows coming into Project Progress that can make it increase (improve) or decrease (get worse).

The story on the right is about the scalability of the project manager. As Project Progress decreases, there is a tendency to add people to a project ("Number of People on the Project" increases). Notice the word "opposite." This means as Project Progress decreases, Number of People does the opposite—it increases. This in turn increases the "Need for PMgr's Time" (as indicated by the word "same"). As the project manager gets caught up in helping the new people, he or she neglects updating the project document. As "Good Project Documentation" decreases, Project Progress decreases as well, because no one knows what's really going on since the documentation is no longer up-to-date.

One of the strongest benefits of Systems Thinking is that it reveals the *mental models* (assumptions) of the participants. In fact, most of the learning that occurs happens in the analysis and creation of the model, not in completing the model. The conversations in building the model will create a strong, shared vision that will allow the team to own the improvement. For example, in the model you saw that as Number of People on the Project decreases, the Need for PMgr's Time decreases as well ("same"). The mental model explains why the group believes this is true, and in this case the mental model is, "As the project manager gets caught up in helping the new people, he or she neglects updating the project document."

To finish reading this model, notice the stories about meetings on the left. As Project Progress decreases, "Bad Meetings" increase ("opposite") due to the stress and pressure that create blame-filled meetings. As there are more Bad Meetings, Project Progress decreases even further (opposite). You can also see that "Good Meetings," when they increase, can increase Project Progress (same). The problem is that as the Need for PMgr's Time increases in times of trouble, Good Meetings decrease (opposite). Notice that Good Meetings and Bad Meetings are two distinct stories—a bad meeting destroys a project; a good meeting improves a project.

Finally, the box that says "Change" is an external factor that can't be controlled by the system, in this case the project. Change happens whether the project has planned for it or not. Change tends most frequently to decrease Project Progress as it increases. Realistically, once the project's progress starts to degrade, many things accelerate the fall.

What can you do then as the project manager? Start by being diligent about preparing for meetings, no matter what. Use minimal documentation like spreadsheet status reports (Chapter 4) and ensure the report is kept up-to-date. Avoid the urge to add people to the project, and add more communication with people already in the know. Causal Loop Diagrams take more time than the other techniques we've looked at, but they illustrate clearly the complexity of a project and the chronic nature of its challenges.

How to Start?

How do you start? Systems Thinking starts with a team that has a vested interest in a complex problem. The diversity of this team is critical to the quality of the results. Unfortunately, the diversity is also directly proportional to the amount of conflict in the analysis process; however, this conflict is needed to move past the obvious and reveal mental models.

The session starts by uncovering the question that the team wants to answer. The participants are asked to create a "why" question. Using "what" and "how" should be avoided because they tend to create questions that suggest a specific problem and solution like, "What happened to the project management workshops?" Some examples of "why" questions are:

Why can't I get through the day without caffeine?

Why don't our sales grow more steadily?

Why do I have to constantly cut price?

Why is it so difficult to keep our skills up-to-date?

Teams discover the power of the initial question time and time again. The question pinpoints the boundaries of the analysis. The question will evolve as the analysis evolves. It is very rare that a team ends up with the same question that they started with. In fact, one of the benefits of Systems Thinking is that it often provokes you to ask questions you hadn't thought to ask.

With practice, teams learn to:

- Recognize the importance of starting with a shared vision by creating a good "why" question
- Recognize loops and validate them against the behavior they observe
- Document delays that cause misdiagnosis and poor intervention
- Document at least one mental model for each influence
- Brainstorm intervention, even on the simplest models, and think through why traditional interventions in these specific situations have failed

Systems Thinking is difficult cognitive work, and when a model is completed it is tempting to just hang it up and move on. However, equal time and creative energy need to be devoted to interventions, since they solve the original problem. We recommend that teams return to the model after a break to talk about intervention.

Systems Thinking allows people to share their unique perspectives and work together. Systems Thinking can be used to facilitate the creation of a shared vision, common mental models, as well as innovative strategies to fix chronic business problems.

Potential Challenges

This approach can get to the problems and successes pretty quickly, but it does not generate discussion around how to change the way things were done to avoid the bad and leverage the good. You may need to have additional conversations and problem solving to translate the problems and benefits into a list of ways to improve.

LEVERAGING THE KNOWLEDGE GAINED

Whether you gather 20 people together to review or you do it quickly yourself while hiding somewhere with free wireless, great benefit will come from pausing to learn. Those in the training industry are well aware of the importance of reflection. The debriefing of case studies is where learning occurs, not the case study itself. Military people are well trained in review. It's how battle strategies are improved. Many industries have a habit of evaluating new products or services. To improve project management competence, you must learn to think about what went well, what didn't go so well, and how you will change going forward.

If you are one of the lucky people who work in a company where you work with others who are trying to improve their project management, then work together to find a way to keep and communicate lessons learned. This can be a simple one-page overview, kept in a shared folder, or a monthly lunch where you share what you've learned that month. Experiment with ways that are best for you to build a strong project management community.

Another organizational option is to create a *peer mentoring* program. The idea is to pair project managers together for three months. During this time, the pair have a monthly meeting where they discuss their current project and challenges. We also add monthly webinars with content and guest speakers for our peer mentors. Leveraging behavioral assessments at the beginning helps the pair connect quickly by honoring communication preferences. To ensure accountability, we use independent coaches to check on the pairs and make sure they are meeting and helping each other as they promised. The meetings can be held face-to-face or virtually.

Today's multitasking, multiproject, multirole work environment makes it more difficult than ever to stop and think before diving into the next adventure. It's hard to even notice that a project has ended before two more have just landed on your desk. Fortunately, the discipline of Review, which we've outlined in this chapter, is tied closely to the discipline of ending.

 Lou's Project Management Diary

Customer Story

I had the opportunity to be part of a large customer project for Ameritech in 1987. The Pan American games were to be held in Indianapolis that summer over a three-week period. A project team representing the five states involved—Indiana, Ohio, Wisconsin, Michigan, and Illinois—was assembled to plan and implement the following:

- Customers would be invited to Indianapolis for three days and two nights. We would provide for their travel, hotel, meals, and sports tickets. In return, they would attend marketing events.

- We would try to the best of our ability to match the customers' preferences for sporting events to the time they would attend.

- Each customer and guest would be paired with a salesperson and guest, and travel, hotel, meals, and sports tickets would be scheduled for the salespeople as well.

- We would create a system to track all of these schedules using personal computers and a "client server" approach.

- Ameritech executives and guests would also be invited and scheduled.

- We would be dedicated to the project full time, starting in early July until the end of August, including living in the hotel we were using for our guests.

Like any project, there were glitches, but overall the customers were unaware. As we "lived" together on the project for weeks on end, away from our families, tensions did arise. There were certainly times when somebody thought somebody else was not pulling their weight. I remember times when we would go to the project manager and demand that he do something about this lack of accountability, but he never did. During the project, I was sure that his was the wrong approach and that it was hindering the project.

A couple of months after the project ended, the team was invited to spend an overnight in Chicago, where we were rewarded with spa visits, sightseeing, dinner, and dancing. They even got us all (even the girls) fitted for tuxes! It was a great time. Before we could go, however, we had to write up a project review.

As I wrote mine, I surprised myself. The very thing that angered me during the project—the project manager's refusal to reprimand inadequate behavior—suddenly looked like the thing that may have led to our success. Our project was complex and needed great resilience. Cell phones were not as prevalent as they are now, and we had to make our own decisions a lot of times because no one else was around. Had the project manager micromanaged every disagreement, the project would have failed.

A little distance on a project changes everything. I learned on this project how important it is to manage a project without micromanaging the people.

SUMMARY CHECKLIST

In this chapter you learned how to:

- Use emotion-based and standard surveys, learning histories, and Systems Thinking to review a project after completion and capture lessons learned

- Create an environment that is blame-free to facilitate actionable lessons from a project review

- Select the most appropriate review technique based on size of the project, conflict during the project, and political importance

- Create an organizational process to capture and share lessons learned to grow overall project management competence

CHAPTER 6

Organizational Change

"It's more fun when you make new mistakes in each project."

In this chapter:

- Apply the Hero's Journey to your project to grow awareness
- Leverage research on leading teams to keep the team aligned
- Apply the Catalyst organizational change process to improve the likelihood of meeting business and project objectives

Lou's Project Management Diary

I was teaching at a client's site the day they did some downsizing. The Human Resources staff prepared me well, and helped me choreograph my breaks so that people could leave class without embarrassment. I knew going into the class that this was going to happen, and the students knew it too. The fear and sadness in the room was palpable as students went to break never to return, not even to pick up their books. By noon, the downsizing was over. The students who remained dutifully returned and tried hard to really learn project management, but kept a close eye on text messages to try to figure out across their office, and the country, who was still there. It was a tremendously sad day. As a company, the downsizing was done "by the book": people were treated fairly, security was high, and people were notified as soon as they could be. However, it wasn't a good day to have people in a class. By the time the powers decided what the date of the layoff would be, it was deemed too late to cancel the class and incur the costs of rescheduling. This lack of coordination between two seemingly unrelated things cost the company money, morale, and an opportunity to learn. Change is never a single event.

Someone in a recent workshop asked me this question: "How do I communicate with my boss that my project workload is unmanageable? I used to work on 30 to 40 projects at a time, but now I'm up to over 100." My workshop attendee's experience is likely familiar to you and is one of the top factors that challenge the success of project managers, a list that includes:

- Unrealistic workloads, constant multitasking, and frequent interruptions

- Ever-present and inadequate technology that work seems to depend on

- Stresses from financial pressures and ongoing unemployment issues

Pretending these factors don't exist just increases the irrational pressure on the project manager to be superhuman. The more pressure, the more stress. The more stress, the more chance of error, rework, and additional stress. It's tough to break the cycle.

In Chapters 2 through 5 you learned how to:

- Start a project well by creating visual documents to create a project charter
- Juggle the work to be done, deadlines, and budget to create a project schedule
- Leverage the project schedule to create timely status emails
- Manage and monitor the project with an eye to how people react to change and how you personally react to stress and frustration
- Review a project and document the learning so projects go better the next time

This chapter will focus on *organizational change*. Projects create change, and as project manager you will have difficulty transitioning a completed project to "live" (up and running) without understanding what prevents people from allowing the change you are introducing to occur.

THE HERO'S JOURNEY

Joseph Campbell was an American professor who studied myths across different cultures and found that they had common patterns of stories woven through them. In his book *The Hero with a Thousand Faces* (available in a volume of collected works published by New World Library, 2008), Campbell wrote about how these patterns of fairy tales are so prevalent in our human psyche that even today our books, movies, and plays still follow the same patterns established thousands of years ago. Projects seem to follow preset story lines and themes, so I think Campbell's insights can teach us a lot about the projects we manage.

Campbell points out that all stories, ancient to modern, involve a hero who faces great challenge and hardship but eventually prevails. Your job as project manager certainly should be considered a heroic journey that is no less difficult than King Author's search for the golden chalice that, when found, will restore the land. Our journey through change follows the patterns shown in Exhibit 6.1.

Notice the circular nature of the pattern. Unlike a Disney movie with a required happy ending, the project manager's hero's journey repeats over and over for as long as the project lasts, and the happy ending is not always assured.

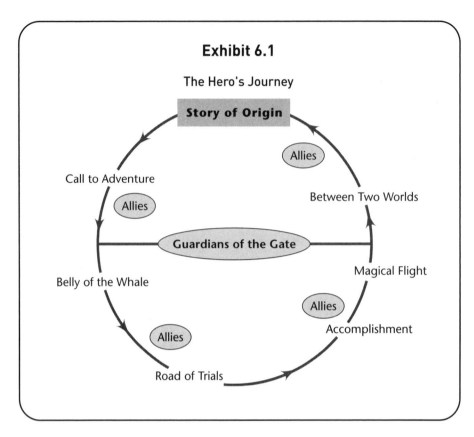

Exhibit 6.1

The Hero's Journey

Story of Origin

Allies

Call to Adventure

Allies

Between Two Worlds

Guardians of the Gate

Belly of the Whale

Magical Flight

Allies

Accomplishment

Allies

Road of Trials

The Story of Origin

Let's begin in the normal world at the start of a project, where everything is exciting and possible. As the project progresses, a little voice inside your head tells you that something is just not right. You can't quite articulate the problem, but you just get this nagging feeling that all is not well.

The Call to Adventure

In your Call to Adventure, you face two things: the pain you feel when you realize that something is wrong with your project and you're no longer willing to ignore it; and the realization that this new problem will force you into a journey out of the nice, status quo world you've relied on. This is your Call to Adventure.

In Campbell's book, many heroes refuse the first Call to Adventure. The hero might be reluctant to see the truth or maybe hopes the issue will go away;

or perhaps doesn't feel competent enough to know what to do. Campbell calls this the *inauthentic state*, because it's inauthentic to believe that you're not good enough to fix the problem or take the journey (that is, your project). As a project manager, it is also inauthentic to believe that you don't have any choice other than failure when the success option appears to have been taken off the table. In fact, for a project manager, "inauthentic" may mean that you aren't willing to accept your role as the hero of this project.

For heroes who refuse the Call to Adventure, one thing always happens: the hero flounders; the hero starts dying inside. But the calls to action keep coming, until one day the hero has no choice but to answer the call, or more accurately, is forced to undertake the Hero's Journey.

Meeting Allies

When the hero commits to the Call to Adventure, an interesting thing happens, according to Campbell's book: Allies appear on the scene as guides. In the project manager's journey, the Ally might give you a special tool, advice, or training to help you face the challenges in your Hero's Journey. You might be offered help with your decisions and help to get through the adventure. Chances are very good that this Ally is not one of the people who were always happy back when you inhabited your Story of Origin. Your project manager adventure may also drive you to seek out someone you think could help.

Crossing the Threshold

The middle line in the diagram is a river to a threshold. As you cross the boundary between your Story of Origin and the unknown world, you are exposed to new learning, surprises, adventures, and experiences you've never had before. You discover aspects about your project or the projects of others that you didn't know. You might also learn that governance is or is not working out as you expected.

As you make these discoveries, you might feel out of place, uncomfortable, and inexperienced. Some part of you may wish that you were back in your ordinary world again. But it's too late. You have to stretch beyond your old self. Many project managers shut down at this point, unable to admit that they have more to learn or need help.

Meeting the Guardians of the Gate

As with Campbell's mythic heroes, you meet resistance when crossing the threshold to knowledge or success. Maybe it is a stakeholder who stands in the way, or perhaps a sponsor has a change of heart. These obstacles are your threshold Guardians, who will test you to see if you're serious about your journey. The Guardians can cause your project to run aground.

The Belly of the Whale

The Guardians are the doubters and naysayers who feed into your lack of confidence. The Guardians are there to test your commitment and to throw all kinds of obstacles, threats, or difficulties in your way to make you back off and go home. You either have to figure out how to overcome these roadblocks or decide that your project is not important. Once you've shown you are committed by doing the necessary hard work, including having tough conversations with the Guardians, you will be allowed passage out of the Belly of the Whale.

It is at this stage on your journey that you have to learn new rules, get comfortable with going to new places, and seeing, hearing, and feeling new things. You must challenge things you always assumed were true. You must ask new questions such as, "How will the project be governed now?" "What will happen to the scope?" "How will the budget and timeline be impacted?"

New Allies

As an emerging hero moving a project forward, you are guaranteed resistance. No matter how obvious the benefit of the project you are trying to complete, someone is going to want something different. Luckily, there are also new Allies at this point to help you understand the new world. Your skills, talents, and abilities are tested and stretched. Every time you surmount resistance, you grow in positive ways. Every time you have a setback, you use the experience to learn and sharpen your game.

The more persistently you move toward the completion of your project, the more you'll attract helpers and Allies who want to help.

Road of Trials

Campbell's mythic heroes eventually face a showdown and test of wills. As project manager, your challenges reach a point that forces you to face them once and for all or risk project and professional failure. The toughest battle you have is with your own self-confidence and commitment.

The feat might be as simple as walking into the office of someone who's been giving you difficulties from Day One and facing that person down. The field of battle might be a phone call from someone you've been avoiding or an in-your-face comment from someone that implies you don't have the skills to manage this project.

The final stage in your growth from an inexperienced, naïve, inauthentic project manager to a true project management hero happens when you face down and overcome your most difficult internal challenges. You'll know when you're at this stage in your project management journey, for it seems the bleakest. Though you can see the end of the project clearly, you realize that the workload is impossible, the deadlines are unattainable, and the budget is blown. In short, you finally understand what a mess you're in. This is the deepest and darkest point in your Hero's Journey.

Accomplishment

Campbell's heroes find untapped resources to meet their challenges. You will find these resources and reasons to succeed as well. Your driver might be a stubborn refusal to let the naysayers win; or maybe you hate the idea of being known as the person who made a mess of an important organizational project. Whatever your reasons for not giving up, you rise above your despair and just go forward.

This unwavering commitment triggers a rush of positive resources that have been with you from the beginning of your Hero's Journey and that bring on the Change. At this point, you are willing to do anything—work long hours, face your worst fears—to succeed. With the rush of new resources strengthening that heroic project manager (that's you), you rise up against despair and overwhelming odds. You face your biggest challenge, brush past your most difficult test, and stretch yourself past every limit in skill and talent you thought you had. You finish the project and go on to claim the well-deserved title of project management hero.

The Magical Flight

You ride off into the sunset in triumph. New Allies think positively about you, and feel you've done well. You take a moment to pause and regroup, but now, like Campbell's hero, you must go back to the Story of Origin.

Between Two Worlds

You have to cross the threshold again, and you are looking forward to returning. But when you return, you are surprised that everything has changed. You are not the person you used to be and neither are the people there. When you look back to the New World from which you have just come, it is no longer a place of uncertainty. You know this New World intimately and have friends and Allies you can count on. You are the master of both worlds, free to journey between both the new and the old. However, don't be surprised if you (the changed you) are not welcomed back by everyone. Luckily, there are new Allies there to help you.

The Next Journey

One of the consequences of your Hero's Journey is the knowledge that life is a series of journeys, and that the end of one journey begets another journey. There's always a few more projects waiting for more of your time.

You probably never really meant to be a project manager. It just sort of happened. And now project management is a big part of your occupation, and it looks like your time on these journeys will only increase. Take a minute to apply this Hero's Journey concept to a project you're involved with right now. Use Sidebar 6.1 to do this work. What kind of insights can you gain to help you to success?

PROJECT LEADERSHIP GROUP DYNAMICS

Wilfred Bion was an influential British psychoanalyst in the mid 1900s. His observations about the role of group dynamics are set out in his book *Experiences in Groups* (Routledge, 1991). Bion identified reoccurring emotional states that groups adopt, which he labeled as assumptions. Although dedicated project teams are rare in today's work environment, even temporary, highly matrixed project teams adopt similar emotions that help or hinder project success.

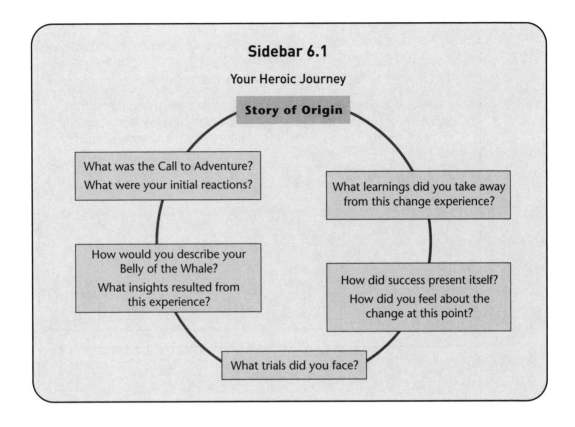

Sidebar 6.1

Your Heroic Journey

Story of Origin

What was the Call to Adventure?
What were your initial reactions?

What learnings did you take away from this change experience?

How would you describe your Belly of the Whale?
What insights resulted from this experience?

How did success present itself?
How did you feel about the change at this point?

What trials did you face?

One of the things that he found was that people hold certain beliefs based on what he called "common ground." Whether it is our family, our work teams, or even our friends, we adopt certain beliefs that influence our choices, especially during a project. If we think that something is going to pull us off this ground, or violate these beliefs, we will fight it in very predictable ways. Use Sidebar 6.2 to think about groups that you are part of and how they influence your beliefs.

A project team is at its best when everyone is working on what they are supposed to be doing. But that can't happen forever. At some point in the project an issue arises that everyone is afraid to deal with. Together, the team will silently agree to not talk about this issue—including the project manager. Use Sidebar 6.3 to think about issues that your project team has been avoiding, and why this might be happening.

Bion identified three basic emotional states that can occur when a group fails to deal with an issue: *dependency*, *fight/flight*, and *pairing*. When a group adopts any one of these states, it interferes with project success dramatically.

In *dependency*, the group draws its confidence and security from the project manager, as in "The project manager will save us." The project team members behave passively, push decisions to the project manager, and act as though the leader has all the answers. Ambitious leaders may like and encourage this role. It's fun to be all-knowing—but it's not realistic. At some point, either resentment from others or an obvious mistake by the project manager will occur. The group will begin to question their confidence in the project manager. This lack of confidence leads the group members to conspire to "take down" the leader, and then search for a new leader. This is a process that is repeated over and over. Think about how many times the first reaction to a troubled project is to bring in a new project manager. Of course, no perfect project manager exists.

When project teams adopt a *fight/flight* emotional state, the team collaborates to preserve itself at all cost. In *fight*, the group may be aggressive and hostile toward other people, especially stakeholders of the project. As discussed above, teams can also fight with the project manager. In *flight*, the group may chit-chat, tell stories, arrive late, or do other things that serve to avoid addressing the task at hand.

Pairing occurs when a project team under stress takes up sides because they are feeling inadequate. Once the team sees that the project manager is flawed and may not be able to "save" them, someone else will step up and attempt to take on the role of leader. The other group members will listen eagerly and attentively with a sense of relief and hopeful anticipation, waiting to see which person wins.

As a project manager, it's pretty normal to take all this personally. It's hard enough to do a project without the team battling you as well. I find it comforting that these patterns of dependency, fight/flight, and pairing occur in almost every group situation to some extent. Being able to think about this behavior as fear rather than the actions of jerks and being courageous enough to talk through the unspoken issues is the best approach.

The worst thing a new project manager can do is pretend he or she has all the answers. The more infallible you pretend to be at the start, the more the team expects you to be. In every project, infallible is not sustainable. Instead, create a team with clear accountabilities and push the problems to the people who should be solving them.

Pat Murray is a consultant and speaker who has studied Bion and works on leveraging these models for stronger leadership and teams. Pat has a three-step process to help a project manager avoid or recover from the dynamics just noted. He recommends:

1. Creating a compelling vision that touches emotions. The business and project objectives are a start on that, but are not sufficient. Consider creating a tagline for the project to rally the troops.

2. Creating a "burning platform." People will rarely trade familiar pain (where you are now) for unfamiliar pain (where you want them to be). You do that by "scaring them with facts," which sends a clear message that "we have to move quickly." This also keeps the team from dependency. Work back from the future for your teams.

3. Creating a logical approach for how to get from A to B. This is where you use dashboards and status reports so that everyone knows who is accountable and for what.

Exhibit 6.2 shares a few recommendations for addressing team issues. Whenever groups of people get together to work on something unstable, conflict can occur. Everyone is sane from their perspective, but together they can create insanity.

Exhibit 6.2

Addressing Group Issues

- Observe rules for governance and good status reporting to hold people accountable
- Stay on track with your business and project objectives
- Know how to lose and gain members with minimal impact
- Bring the real issues to the team—no meetings after the meeting
- Value each member
- Demand that each member face and cope with stress and discontent openly

---

A PROCESS FOR ORGANIZATIONAL CHANGE

Many project managers focus entirely on the project tasks and ignore the need to address the organizational resistance that comes with any change. A lack of communication creates certain failure for a project. Engagement leads to buy-in, which in turn unleashes passion and drives results.

Chip Neidigh, www.catalystoc.com, has a simple, clean, and powerful model for organizational change. The Catalyst Change Model recognizes the importance of engagement (by leaders and staff) throughout an organizational change. His process emphasizes the need for communication and training as part of any project plan. I have personally worked with him on very difficult projects that have succeeded using this strategy. Exhibit 6.3 shows his approach.

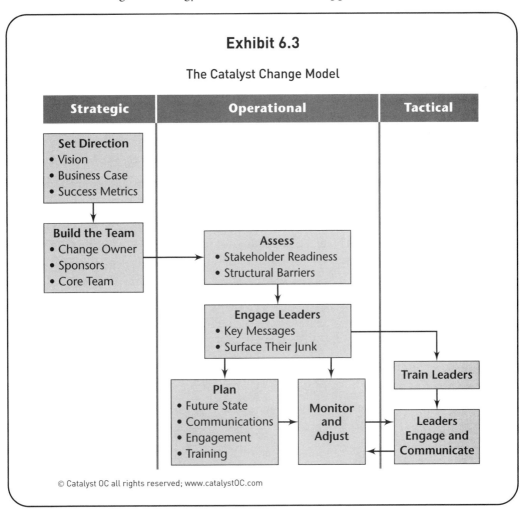

Exhibit 6.3

The Catalyst Change Model

© Catalyst OC all rights reserved; www.catalystOC.com

This model provides a flexible structure for managing change. The three levels of change management reflect the different roles of the stakeholders during change initiatives:

Strategic. A change project begins by empowering a select group to define strategy, make the business case, and charter project teams

Operational. Senior leaders and a "core team" of project resources are responsible for change planning and course adjustments "on the ground"

Tactical. Frontline leaders play a critical role in executing the change plan

Throughout the project, key messages communicate and manage the expectations of each of the three groups of stakeholders. Chip uses this simple checklist to construct messages that work:

- Where are we going?

- Why are we doing this?

- How much is this going to hurt?

- What do you expect of me?

- What support and help will I get?

Exhibit 6.4 shows a copy of a change readiness assessment that Chip also likes to use to assess how much organizational change management will be required when an initiative kicks off.

To create alignment to the change requires a unifying statement of purpose. Use Sidebar 6.4 to create a tagline for your project.

Exhibit 6.4

Organizational Change Assessment

Organizational Change Assessment

This assessment assumes that the respondent is in an organization with a disruptive change that is under way (or will be soon). It may be beneficial to capture the opinions of multiple individuals within your organization to generate a broader understanding of strengths to leverage and challenges to overcome.

Instructions:
1. Please mark your level of agreement with each statement.
2. Calculate the numerical average for each section and record it. Lower averages indicate challenges that may impede the success of the change effort.

Section I: **Leadership**		strongly disagree	disagree	neutral	agree	strongly agree
1	We have the right leaders in place to ensure the change is a success.	①	②	③	④	⑤
2	Executives demonstrate (in words and actions) support for the change.	①	②	③	④	⑤
3	Front-line managers demonstrate (in words and actions) support for the change.	①	②	③	④	⑤
4	Our leaders listen to employee concerns about the change and are able to adequately address them.	①	②	③	④	⑤
5	Our leaders are effective and they work well together.	①	②	③	④	⑤
				Section Average:		

Section II: **Communication**		strongly disagree	disagree	neutral	agree	strongly agree
6	Employees have a clear vision of what the organization will look like after the change.	①	②	③	④	⑤
7	Our leaders are unified and aligned in their communications about this change.	①	②	③	④	⑤
8	Employees receive accurate information about the change.	①	②	③	④	⑤
9	Employees receive timely information about the change.	①	②	③	④	⑤
10	Communication about the change is clear and easy to understand.	①	②	③	④	⑤
				Section Average:		

(continued)

(continued)

Section III: **Planning and Support**	strongly disagree	disagree	neutral	agree	strongly agree
11	It is clear how we will measure success in this change.	①	②	③	④	⑤
12	We are appropriately staffing this change to ensure its success.	①	②	③	④	⑤
13	We are appropriately funding this change to ensure its success.	①	②	③	④	⑤
14	We will get all the technical support we need to make this change a success.	①	②	③	④	⑤
15	The plan to implement the change will ensure that important daily work still gets done.	①	②	③	④	⑤
				Section Average:	

Section IV: **Risk Mitigation**	strongly disagree	disagree	neutral	agree	strongly agree
16	We have identified all the major risks that threaten the change's success.	①	②	③	④	⑤
17	We have defined mitigation strategies for all the major risks we have identified.	①	②	③	④	⑤
18	We clearly understand how this change will negatively impact customers.	①	②	③	④	⑤
19	We clearly understand how this change will negatively impact employees.	①	②	③	④	⑤
20	We clearly understand how this change will negatively impact suppliers.	①	②	③	④	⑤
				Section Average:	

Section V: **Engagement**	strongly disagree	disagree	neutral	agree	strongly agree
21	Employees believe that this change is necessary.	①	②	③	④	⑤
22	All employees who will be affected by the change understand what the change is.	①	②	③	④	⑤
23	Employees' opinions count in determining how the change will be implemented.	①	②	③	④	⑤
24	Employees' roles in the change are clear to them.	①	②	③	④	⑤
25	Employees actively help other employees get committed to the change.	①	②	③	④	⑤
				Section Average:	

Combining the Hero's Journey, Bion's work with teams, and Chip's work with organizational change creates a systemic approach to driving project success. Clarity around your own journey, the journey of the project team, and the journey of the organizational stakeholders will help you get your arms around this nebulous villain called change. Using Sidebar 6.5, take a minute to turn your organizational change ideas into project tasks for your current project. Do this before you move on.

Lou's Project Management Diary Customer Story

Recently, I had the privilege to work with Chip on a corporate acquisition project/change. A relatively small, city-owned utility company would be acquiring the city water company from a for-profit vendor, as well as wastewater and some other assets. Over the years, pieces of the water company organization had been bounced around, sold, and resold. Nothing like that had ever happened at the acquiring utility company; the family-like atmosphere fostered teamwork and trust.

As part of the motivation for the city to allow this acquisition to occur, there was a large dollar benefit to reducing the workforce through combining the organizations. The staff at the utility company initially felt somewhat sad for the people who would lose their jobs at the acquired companies. Later on, they would discover that there would be downsizing at all organizations.

Chip's company was hired to drive the organizational change. Both cultures would be changed. Both companies would experience a staff reduction. Once the utility commission said go (if they did), there would be very little time to convert everything and everybody to one company. Special project teams had been built for the integration. New roles were created, but people were still expected, for the most part, to do their "real" jobs in parallel. There were a lot of unknowns, lots of political confusion, and lots of pressure.

Through coaching, messaging, training, and constant reinforcement, Chip helped the leaders keep the messages clear, consistent, and timely. Some decisions weren't liked, but they weren't a surprise. There was dependency, fight/flight, and pairing, just like there always is. There were issues that were not initially talked about until Chip helped the appropriate leader go after it.

When the weekend finally came to integrate the companies over a period of just a few days, it went quietly and efficiently. No drama. No headlines. It was amazing.

Do not underestimate the power of organizational change done well, or the terror of organizational change ignored.

SUMMARY CHECKLIST

In this chapter you learned how to:

- See your project manager role as the role of a hero, and identify with the trials and joys of that journey.

- Notice when teams begin to behave in ways that avoid work. Issue resolution to return to work is the role of the project manager.

- Apply an organizational change model like the Catalyst Change Model to your project to ensure that your messaging is consistent, timely, and truthful.

CHAPTER 7

Organizational Project Management

"Saying 'we'll do it!' in a meeting is verifying that you have no intention of doing it nor does anyone else."

In this chapter:

- Differentiate between personal and organizational project management
- Define the roles and processes of a project management office (PMO)
- Create a project plan to migrate to a project management office
- Identify options for an organizational project dashboard
- Identify technology options for implementing a strong project portfolio process

The same "aha" moment occurs in most of the workshops we conduct when members of an established team get a chance to review the scope diagrams of the other teams. Invariably, someone will comment, "Wow, I thought my project was going to be tough to get done with my current workload, but I just noticed that I'm also a stakeholder on everybody else's project." It's one of those obvious facts of life that you don't necessarily notice until you think about it in today's work environment of multitasking and shared resources: you are pretty much guaranteed to be needed on many other projects—some you don't even know about.

This is a critical leadership challenge. Without a dashboard of current projects that includes milestone due dates and tasks owned by key stakeholders, it is impossible to manage the capacity of teams and the organization as a whole. Ignoring capacity problems (not enough people for the work to be done in the time planned) always results in poor-quality deliverables, the result of an overstressed staff contending heroically with massive rework issues.

Project management leadership is all about aligning the right people and resources required to meet your business objectives. As the project manager, you must keep your eye on the big picture to ensure that strategic and project quality goals for your business are met. To do this requires a standard documentation approach that improves the success of individual projects while scaling up into an organizational portfolio of projects for management decision making. In many cases, organizations fail to create (1) a scalable individual approach to managing projects, or (2) an efficient dashboard approach at the organizational level. That is, the approach that is used just adds more work to overstressed individual projects. You'll need to design an approach that meets both goals. This organizational project dashboard is usually called the Project Management Office (PMO).

 Lou's Project Management Diary

One of our customers with a large training organization decided to invest in training for operations, including safety, compliance, and sales topics related to their consumer-facing stores. Each learning experience was created through collaboration with multiple stakeholders, including subject-matter experts from the operations area. Quite often the request from the business for training had an urgency component, which was perfectly logical considering the safety, compliance, and sales focus. However, the subject-matter experts' real job was supporting operations, so their sense of urgency did not usually match the urgency of the training developers. Pushed, the training developers had to make their best content guess and move on.

When user testing began, these content guesses often resulted in lots of rework since assumptions had to be made to make the aggressive due dates. The company estimated that it cost almost $3,000 every time a training development project went through another rework cycle, and most projects had a number of rework incidents. The solution to this problem was to institute a standard approach to course development that ensured the right requirements were gathered as early as possible.

Although a standard approach is a great idea, and can significantly shorten the struggle of those beginning a new project, it did not improve the subject-matter experts' sense of urgency. Instead, it added a "learning curve" to the already overworked lives of developers. Clearly, the solution to reducing rework needed an *organizational agreement* on the urgency, not merely more standardization procedures for the training staff. The operations project sponsors were putting out aggressive and unattainable dates resulting in their staff missing required project timelines. Using a standard approach did point out the project stall points; however, it took organizational commitment to clarify accountability.

In Chapters 2 and 3, you learned how to successfully start and plan a project by creating visual documents of the following conversations:

- Business objectives (IRACIS)
- Scope diagram
- Project objectives

- Risks and mitigation

- Constraints

- Governance plan

- Communications plan

- Project schedule: tasks/milestones, people, dependencies, due dates

Then in Chapters 4 and 5, you learned the importance of managing, ending, and reviewing projects. In Chapter 6, you learned important ways to build project tasks that help your stakeholders through the changes brought on by the project. All the deliverables discussed in these chapters increase the likelihood that your project will be successful with a limited amount of rework and frustration.

Take a look at Exhibit 7.1. You will recognize the project management model introduced in Chapter 1. As you remember, it consists of these four phases:

Define answers the question *why*

Plan answers the question *how*

Manage requires seeking to *adapt*

Review requires seeking to *learn*

This chapter will focus on combining these individual project plans into one organizational planning tool.

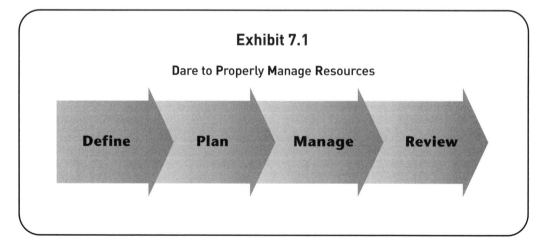

Exhibit 7.1

Dare to Properly Manage Resources

Define   Plan   Manage   Review

DIFFERENTIATE BETWEEN PERSONAL AND ORGANIZATIONAL PROJECT MANAGEMENT

Before we learn more about creating an organizational approach, let's review the difference between personal and organizational project management (at least as I define it). *Personal project management* is a repeatable process with techniques and tools that you use to plan, organize, and manage all of your projects. Alumni of our books and workshops implement small to large versions of this repeatable process. Personal project management maturity ranges from someone who occasionally sketches out a project schedule (low maturity) to someone who creates and monitors all the techniques (and sometimes more!) in this book (high maturity). Low-maturity project management has value, but in the scheme of things, high-maturity project management has more value. However, be aware that high-maturity project management carries with it the danger of your spending too much time on the nuts and bolts of project management, which is just as bad as doing nothing.

Organizational project management is a big-picture view of all the projects that are being *invested* in by the business (all projects cost money). Organizational project management includes timelines, budgets, resource needs, and of course business and project objectives. Depending on the number of concurrent projects, the organization may decide to just track projects over a certain budget amount—projects that have the highest risk or highest return. This criterion for tracking projects needs to be tested and adjusted over time. In a pinch, every overworked project manager modifies the timeline or budget to slip under the radar of the PMO and avoid dealing with what is perceived as useless bureaucracy.

In this book, I'm focusing on smaller team and functional area organizational PMOs, not enterprise, company-wide, or global PMOs. For more information on enterprise PMOs, I recommend the work of Randy Englund, especially *Creating the Project Office: A Manager's Guide to Leading Organizational Change* by Englund, Paul Dinsmore, and Bob Graham (Jossey-Bass, 2003).

It is very unlikely that organizational project management will be successful if those doing the individual projects are not motivated to improve their individual project success. Thankfully, most are. As a project manager, you know that time management is a prerequisite for good project management; and as you might suspect, being adept at the personal level is an important prerequisite for effective organizational project management.

When a leader decides to create a project management office and doesn't clearly share the reason for it, it is unlikely to be successful. The staff usually resists because the business and project objectives of the initiative are not clear. And the project is usually seen by overworked project managers as just another pile of work to do. Worst case, the PMO is seen as an auditor, a surefire kiss of death for the project. If on the other hand the leader is hearing cries for help from his or her team about resource availability and project interdependencies, and leverages this information to build a PMO, the success rate is improved. You'll read more about improving the adoption of a PMO process below. As you learned in the last chapter, change—even potentially good change—is unsettling.

DEFINE THE ROLES AND PROCESSES OF A PROJECT MANAGEMENT OFFICE

Unfortunately, the term *project management office* implies that it is a physical location. One of the worst things you can do to begin a PMO is create a snazzy physical location (a tricked-out conference room, for example) and have a flashy open house so everyone can come visit. This ensures that every project failure going forward will be blamed on the PMO—it's like drawing a giant bull's-eye on your back. In more successful cases, the term is used to describe a role or job description, not a place or function.

The role or roles of a PMO are more successful when defined as an internal consultant or resource rather than as someone in a controlling role. Most successful PMOs see their role as a knowledge-exchange resource. The PMO team leader's role is to pay attention (more than anyone else) to the big picture of all the projects in an organization. With a big-picture view, the PMO is able to connect a project manager to work that's already done and to connect others on the team to expertise and resources they may not know about.

In a smaller organization, the PMO is part of someone's job. For example, the clinical training organization of a hospital may ask the staff administrator to play the role of the PMO. In the hierarchy of the organization, this role falls below the role of most project managers, so it's a somewhat unusual example compared to our general perspective of a PMO leader. On the other hand, the staff administrator is probably the best project manager in the department!

This arrangement is advantageous because this person is already aware of the organizational big picture and likely excels at detail work and communication. In larger organizations, the PMO may consist of a team of dedicated staff, including a leader and a team of internal consultants. Notice that the emphasis is on supporting others versus controlling others.

Exhibit 7.2 contains some job criteria for a PMO role.

Exhibit 7.2

The Role of the Project Management Office

The project management office (PMO) role may contain all or some of the following responsibilities:

- Update and maintain an organizational view of the project portfolio, including:

    Status

    Roles

    Priority

    Business and project objectives

    Stakeholders

    Governance

- Communicate organizational project status to leadership and key stakeholders
- Troubleshoot accidental project overlaps, resource contention, and gaps
- Identify redundant or shared work opportunities between projects
- Support the use of individual and/or organizational technology to share project artifacts
- Recommend ways to improve overall project management processes

---

Here is how all the roles work together:

- The PMO owns the support and maintenance of the process and technological dashboard

- The leader(s) of the organization own the governance of the projects
- The project managers, of course, are accountable for the success of the projects they manage

CREATE A PROJECT PLAN TO MIGRATE TO A PROJECT MANAGEMENT OFFICE

The irony of project management is that the bigger the deal you make of the new standard PMO and process in your company, the less likely people will want to adopt your approach. Consider these words used frequently to describe organizational project management:

- A *standard* approach
- A dashboard for *control*
- An *audit* of our project

None of the words in italics create hope and excitement in a project manager. Each of these words implies that there will be layers of overhead added to the already ambitious projects people are working on, making it more and more likely that projects will be late and over budget. Avoid teeing up your approach with these types of words.

Here are some of the wrong reasons to create an organizational approach to project management:

- To treat every project the same way
- To make sure everyone is doing projects the same way
- To insert a process that replaces the need for people to come up with their own solutions
- Because everyone else has a PMO and we don't

Here are great reasons to create an organizational project management approach:

- To reduce rework. If someone else has figured out a scope diagram for a large e-learning development project, why not start with that rather than start from scratch?
- To make sure we aren't lying to ourselves about capacity. How can leaders tell when their project staff is full or overloaded? This is critical because overload creates project churn-and-burn.

- To connect silos. Sharing a language for what you need from other stakeholders in the company increases the accuracy of communication and reduces chaos.

- To identify redundant projects. In large organizations, variations of the same project can be chartered without anyone knowing. Doing a project once instead of multiple times naturally avoids cost and frees resources for other work.

Implementing a PMO successfully is a project, not a task. It is all about the design and creation of a repeatable process. You'll remember from Chapter 1 that we talked about the difference between a task, a process, and a project. Developing and transitioning to a PMO is a *project*; the ongoing execution and maintenance of the PMO is a *process*. Before you jump into creating a PMO, follow the same steps you learned in Chapters 1 through 6 (especially the change-management aspects). We'll start with Define.

Define

The most important business objective of a PMO is improved efficiencies, which means it's an Avoid Cost project, primarily. For example, the business objective might be something like:

The PMO will avoid cost to the organization by increasing the alignment of projects to critical business goals, which will decrease rework and improve the quality of the project deliverables.

The project sponsor of the PMO is normally the leader of the organization being served by the PMO.

The project objectives need to be well thought-out. These are the "promises" of what the PMO will deliver. What do you think about the following project objective? How would you feel to hear it?

When implemented, the PMO will monitor the milestones of all projects with a budget of over $25,000 or a timeline of over six months.

Although often a critical function of a PMO, this sounds like policing. If you are building a new PMO process, be aware that you are bringing a large change to your staff (see the previous chapter for tips). Consider the impact your project charter's wording will have on managing expectations. It would probably be better to lead this objective with:

The PMO will provide resources to organizational project managers and partner with them to improve their projects' success.

Here are some verbs that might be handy when you define the project objectives (the "promises") of your new PMO:

Troubleshoot

Establish (a repeatable process)

Transition (to a repeatable process)

Support

Communicate

Research (best practices)

Grow (project management competence)

When you draw a scope diagram of your new PMO, include some or all of these stakeholders:

Project manager (whom does the PMO see as its customers?)

Enterprise PMO (if there are other PMOs it makes sense to align with)

IT (for support of the technology component of your PMO, if needed)

Project Management Institute (if this is critical to your organization)

Training (if the PMO will own training on the process)

Process owner (whoever will own the final process)

Use Sidebar 7.1 to sketch out a quick scope diagram (see Chapter 2) for a PMO in your organization.

Sidebar 7.1

Drawing a Scope Diagram for Your PMO

Take a minute to apply what you learned in Chapter 2 to a PMO project for your organization. If you already have a PMO, use this diagram to see if you are missing any stakeholders right now in your existing process. If you do not have a PMO, use this diagram to begin to think about the scope of the change you will be undertaking. Make sure it's commensurate with the value you will get back.

Establishing a PMO can be a risky endeavor, so take a good look at the risks that have occurred when other new processes have been rolled out in your organization, successfully or not. Exhibit 7.3 shows a list of common risks for new PMOs.

Exhibit 7.3

Risks of a Project Management Office

- *Inconsistent sponsorship or lack of governance.* Avoiding this requires a tough project sponsor keeping a solid eye on business and project objectives.

- *Analysis paralysis.* In creating a PMO process, especially by a committee made up of people with too many tactical responsibilities, momentum can be lost. Consider hand-picking one or two project managers to create a sample process (or grab someone else's from the web), ask for feedback, then implement. The process will change anyway as you start using it, so don't expect it to be perfect from the start.

- *Too much detail.* Avoid the "control" mentality as much as possible. Keep the process broad and the tools simple to ensure quicker buy-in at rollout.

- *Taking too long.* Once you decide to build a PMO, get it up and running quickly. If you work on it for too long, you'll lose the moment of need.

- *No resources.* After implementation to maintain and evolve the PMO.

Ideally, creating a PMO should have the following constraints:

	No More	Little More	Negotiate
Time		X	
Cost	X		
Quality/Scope			X

No More Money: do it as cheaply as possible
Little More Time: roll out quickly
Negotiate Scope: do a simple process well

Now turn to your organization, in Sidebar 7.2, to create your PMO deliverables.

Sidebar 7.2

Your PMO Deliverables

Complete the project charter for a PMO for your organization here. Include the following deliverables you learned about in Chapter 2:

- Business objectives (prioritized)
- Project objectives
- Scope diagram (you just did this)
- Quick and Dirty Risk Assessment number and risk mitigation table
- Constraints
- Communications plan
- Governance plan

Plan, Manage, Review, and Change

Build your project plan just like any other, using milestones if that makes sense. This will drive the communication you will need if you are to maintain the buy-in of your sponsor and organization. As you learned in Chapter 6, managing organizational change requires lots of clean, basic, honest communication. Communicate the status of the PMO early and often. Stay on the radar of the organization and model the great project management behaviors you'd like to make a regular occurrence.

IDENTIFY OPTIONS FOR AN ORGANIZATIONAL PROJECT DASHBOARD

The best way to identify options for an organizational dashboard is to put yourself in the place of a leader heading up an organization full of people juggling multiple projects. From this leader's perspective, what information would be useful to you? What gauges would this leader like to have available on his or her dashboard? Work with the project sponsor to get a sense of the answers to these questions.

Do not start this process by thinking up things you can measure. This is a very common mistake. Often people measure things that are easy to measure instead of what's important to measure. Here are some common questions the PMO and leadership will have about the organization's projects:

- Is the dashboard data for each project up-to-date?

- What is the current status of each project in terms of timeline and budget?

- What are the three critical issues constraining each project's progress? How can the PMO help?

- What are the critical cross-project dependencies, and are the dates sane? For example, is the IT hardware work going to be done in time to install the new training platform?

- How does the future implementation of the project objectives for all projects look? Will there be resource constraints at implementation time that could be avoided with a little adjustment? Are there issues with people rolling off projects too late or too early?

- When was the last time each project manager talked with the project sponsor? In other words, are the customers of each project still happy?

Turn to your organization, in Sidebar 7.3, to think about your PMO project plan.

Sidebar 7.3

Your PMO Project Plan

Think about what the milestones would be for implementing a PMO in your organization. Create a schedule of the due dates and dependencies for each milestone. Add tasks between the milestones and figure out how much help you will need. Remember to consider the change-management aspects and what communications you will need to help people adopt the PMO process.

In the classic project management book *The Mythical Man Month*, Frederik Brooks posed and answered the question, "How does a project get one year late? One day at a time." It is easy for the PMO to begin to slip into an auditing role. To reiterate, the PMO owns the availability and maintenance of the dashboard once it is created; the leaders own the governance of the projects. The project managers, of course, are accountable for the success of the projects they manage. The auditor role is tempting to the ego. However, when trouble appears on the dashboard, the leader of the organization must work with the project manager to mitigate the situation. The PMO is available as a resource to help improve the project process.

In Exhibits 7.4 and 7.5, you'll see two very different examples of project dashboard components created by Trish Uhl, www.accidentalprojectmanager.com.

Exhibit 7.4 is a more traditional project dashboard, using stoplight colors to quickly identify what is going well, what is completed, and what is in trouble or getting close to it. Notice that this dashboard emphasizes looking forward, not figuring out whose fault it was that things are off track. The focus on what is most important right now is a powerful way to keep everyone engaged in the process. Page two provides the drill-down detail to see specifically where the issues are and who owns them.

The dashboard in Exhibit 7.5 is an even more strategic take on a project. This keeps everyone's eyes on the five drivers of success identified early in the project. It is a larger view of a project's progress independent of dates. This might be a good addition to the more traditional dashboard, and it might be more pertinent to the project manager and stakeholders than the project sponsor.

Exhibit 7.4

Traditional Project Dashboard

Project Dashboard

Status Key:

Project Charter Summary

Deliverable	Details
Project Sponsor	Jon Smith 555-1212 jxmith@somewhere.com
Project Manager	Lee Franz 555-1213 lkfrainz@somewhere.com
Primary Business Objective	Increase revenue through more effective marketing initiatives
Project Objectives	Create measurable and detailed project plans for every marketing initiative (treat as projects). Track actual cost of marketing to return at eighteen month intervals to adjust strategy as the year progresses.
Stakeholders	Project Sponsor, Sales, It Training, Customers, Strategic Vendors

Project Plan: Milestone Analysis due 6/1

Task	Owner	Actual Expense	Mar	Apr	May	Jun	Jul	Aug	Status	Comments
Complete the products requirement definition document	Tom	$1,500	▨	▨						**Complete.** Task was in progress for two months and finished at the end of April.
Review with product development team; gather feedback; incorporate feedback	Tom	$400			▨	▨				Tom has set up a meeting with the team next week.
Give document to product development for prototype development	Michelle	$500			▨	▨				Michelle on unexpected medical leave, so we need to work around her absence. We will be able to complete this task, but we need to make sure that the schedule doesn't slip.
Total Expense:		$2,400								
Total Elapse Time:	3 Months									
Dependencies on:	Project Charter Approval									
Dependencies for:	Milestone DESIGN									
General comments:	Initial feedback from product development team was very positive—things are looking good!									

Exhibit 7.5

More Strategic Project Dashboard

Status Key:
- On track (green)
- Minor glitches that need attention but will not delay the deliverable (yellow)
- Major glitches that need attention and will (or most likely will) delay the deliverable (red)

Top Five Action Items to Address Drivers

Driver	Action Description	Status	Status Description	Owner	Original Due Date	Current Due Date
Process Gaps: Gaps identified and documented for future state policies, process, and procedures	Identify and document gaps. Schedule process walkthroughs with process owners.	On track	Fifteen gaps identified and reviewed. Walkthroughs complete with ten processes.	Patty	7/28	7/28
Training Readiness: Lack of team alignment on expected outcomes, key messages, content	Revisit compelling reasons for completing the project by reviewing requirements and performance metrics with team.	Problem	Difficulty getting team to refocus, escalated to executive sponsor, who will provide clarification at upcoming team meeting.	Charlie	8/25	9/9
Training Strategy: Power users not identified	Socialize power user charter with business leads and ask for resource assignments.	Caution	Difficulty getting on agendas for two business leads, escalated to executive sponsor who will schedule meetings.	Charlie	7/21	7/30
Training Strategy: Business users not as PC savvy as anticipated	Explore options for quickly improving business users' PC skills.	On track	Developing detailed PC skills training plan, investigating funding options.	Charlie	8/1	8/1
Training Curriculum: Vendor is late delivering materials	Review and approve vendor's corrective action plan.	Caution	Corrective action plan in place.	Linus	7/22	8/1

IDENTIFY TECHNOLOGY OPTIONS FOR IMPLEMENTING A STRONG PROJECT PORTFOLIO PROCESS

Watch out for spending too much time messing with technology. As always, it is more important that you have a clear idea what you are tracking and why than what technology you will use. Certainly the right technology can maximize communication, sharing, lessons learned, and even maintenance of the process, but looking for *perfect* technology is a Don Quixote kind of experience.

The minute you type up a list there will be new tools available, so head to the web and search for what others are using. Don't invent a project dashboard; search for examples of what others are doing and how. When considering tools, remember that there is a difference between individual, organizational, and enterprise project management. Be sure you know what you want the tool *to do* before you get dazzled by bells and whistles. Simplicity and alignment to your process are key decision criteria.

To create an organizational dashboard, you'll have to merge information from the individual projects into one "thing." You can merge information by hand, or you can try to find or build a tool to automate the merge, which of course will be more complicated and expensive.

Here are some of the current tools that my clients have used for their organizational PMOs:

MS Excel. Trish Uhl's sample dashboards in the previous section are Excel-based, and are shared through a web portal and/or Sharepointe (see next page). Many of our customers use Excel this way. Most people already have the software and at some level know how to use it.

MS Project. This tool has the capability to link smaller projects together for tracking at a high (or low) level and has great reports for tracking resources. The downside is that its power comes at the cost of complexity. If you do use MS Project (or MS Project Server as a shared platform), I'd recommend that you make one person the project administrator responsible for creating reports, and keep your project teams from losing themselves in the tool. Build the expertise in a few people rather than minimal expertise with lots of struggle in all your project management staff.

Basecamp. This is an example of a simple-to-use web (cloud) tool. It tracks tasks, people, and duration/dates. With the right passwords, you can share project plans. However, it is set up more for individual rather than organizational project management.

Google Docs. If you have someone with the right expertise, you can use Google Docs to share spreadsheets and other project documents on the web. The interface, however, is not the same as what most people are used to.

Collaboration Software/Space. Using a tool like Wordpress or Squidoo to create a virtual community for sharing documents is a way to share project documentation.

MS Sharepointe. This enterprise software creates both a shared space for documents as well as some shared scheduling. You probably already have it.

 Lou's Project Management Diary

One of my favorite PMOs is at McDonald's US. The IT department has created a set of Excel tools that are available and shareable through a web portal to track as much or as little of your personal and organizational projects as you choose. Although these tools were originally set up for IT projects and have been adopted deeply there, the staff of the IT PMO sees its role as "helper" for anyone at McDonald's who wants to get better at project management. The staff is frequently showing up to help other areas of the company adapt the IT tools to a repeatable yet simple way to do and track projects. There is no "hard sell" or threat of escalation if people choose not to use these tools. The use of these "spreadsheets on steroids" has grown organically, because the PMO staff has approached its role with a servant-leader mentality.

SUMMARY CHECKLIST

In this chapter you learned how to:

- Differentiate between personal, organizational, and enterprise project management

- Define the roles and processes of a project management office (PMO), emphasizing knowledge sharing and project management capacity building

- Apply everything you've learned in earlier chapters to create a project charter and project plan to migrate to a PMO as quickly as possible, with plans to evolve it over time

- Create a project dashboard by identifying first what the organizational leadership and project managers need to know to ensure that projects are aligned to the priorities of the business

- Identify options for an organizational project dashboard

- Identify the best technology options for implementing a strong project portfolio process for the needs of your organization, and avoid spending too much time looking for the perfect app

CHAPTER 8

Insanity Is Just a Project Constraint

"Think of projects as flash mobs. People share a purpose, have clear roles, show up, surprise everyone, then disappear. No wonder our stakeholders don't like to see us coming."

You can always learn more project management processes and techniques. The PMBOK (Project Management Body of Knowledge) changes almost every year, and best practices continue to evolve. The missing concept that drives my perspective is that there is a huge difference between project management as a career—for example, on my business card—and managing projects as part of my "real job." That's what I do, and I'm pretty sure that's what most of you do as well.

With that assumption, here are a few tips to help you ease comfortably into the world of project management. You've invested some amount of time in this book, even if it was just the time you took to buy it. You took a step towards action. Here are some ways to get the ROI that you deserve by focusing on your own growth:

1. Be really clear who the project sponsor is. Really clear. Don't let other people convince you that the missing sponsor will show up, no big deal. It is a *really* big deal. If possible, meet with the project sponsor face-to-face, no matter how little time you get.

2. Think about your role as project manager as one of the many roles you juggle in your life. The people who meet you when you are playing the role of parent would certainly describe you differently from the people who meet you when you are in your role at work. Think about the person you become when you play the PM role. Give yourself time to embrace that role, just like you would the other important roles in your life. Just like parenting, it is easy to avoid the project management role when things get tough. Fight the urge.

3. Force the discussion about the business objectives. No one will want to talk about it, and many will tell you it's obvious. Minimally, establish whether the primary goal is to make money or drive out cost.

4. I am really biased toward the project scope diagram. I know it's a little weird looking and seems like a big change, but try one for just one of your projects and notice what happens. You have a powerful tool in your tool chest now, so don't leave it there. Even if you're too chicken to show it to other people, just draw one for yourself. Your project will benefit greatly.

5. Set up the project objectives. No one will want you to do this, because that eliminates a lot of wiggle room. It will be much harder for your stakeholders to say, "Oh yeah, I'm sure I told you we needed that ..." Change will still occur, but everyone will agree that the project has indeed changed.

6. Work back from the delivery date. Put your tasks in a spreadsheet and work out one person who is responsible for each task and when it is due. Don't get sidetracked or enamored with powerful project management software until you have practiced with the training wheels of a spreadsheet. Put another way, learn to plan a project well first before you dive into the deep end of a complicated tool.

7. Remind everyone of their responsibilities by sharing your little spreadsheet on a regular basis, probably once a week or so. Do this predictably and your team will think you rock. They will respect your organizational skills and will help you.

8. Do a review of your project even if you just do it by yourself. Even better, keep a project journal somewhere so you can capture lessons learned as you go.

9. Hold as much time as possible to work on projects. Work in big chunks. Keep your head down, no distractions. Multitasking is the evil enemy of project success. Overload and chaos are the underlings of multitasking.

10. Laugh. Projects are ridiculously funny. It's amazing what we can accomplish given the crazy things that are asked of us by seemingly sane people. The world is funny; enjoy it.

If you've taken my advice about reading the chapters as you need them, you have arrived at this page on a very depressing day, with feelings of incompetence and frustration. If you've read the entire book cover to cover, you may already be an effective project manager. Either way, here is a little joke to hold you up and show you that projects are crazy but that project managers who are resilient and adaptive will ultimately be successful.

Three project managers and three accountants are traveling by train to a big meeting at headquarters to discuss efficiencies. At the station, the three accountants each buy tickets and watch as the three project managers buy only a single ticket. "How are three people going to travel on only one ticket?" asks an accountant. "Watch and you'll see," answers a project manager.

They all board the train. The accountants take their respective seats, but all three project managers cram into a very small restroom and close the door behind them. Shortly after the train has departed, the conductor comes around collecting tickets.

He knocks on the restroom door and says, "Ticket, please." The door opens just a crack and a single arm emerges with a ticket in hand. The conductor takes it and moves on.

The accountants see this and agree it was quite a clever idea. So after the big meeting, the accountants decide to copy the project managers on the return trip and save some money. After all, the big meeting had been about efficiencies!

When they get to the station, they buy a single ticket for the return trip. To their astonishment, the project managers buy no tickets at all.

"How are you going to travel without a ticket?" says one perplexed accountant. "Watch and you'll see," answers a project manager.

When they board the train, the three accountants cram into a restroom and the three project managers cram into another restroom nearby. The train departs. Shortly afterward, one of the project managers leaves his restroom and walks over to the restroom where the accountants are hiding. He knocks on the door and says, "Ticket, please."

ABOUT THE AUTHOR

Lou Russell is the CEO of Russell Martin & Associates and an executive consultant, speaker, and author, whose passion is to create growth in companies by guiding the growth of their people. In her speaking, training, and writing, Lou draws on 30 years of experience helping organizations achieve their full potential. She is committed to inspiring improvement in all three sides of what she has dubbed the Optimization Triangle: leadership, project management, and individual learning.

Lou is the author of six popular and practical books: *IT Leadership Alchemy, The Accelerated Learning Fieldbook, Training Triage, Leadership Training, Project Management for Trainers,* and *10 Steps to Successful Project Management.* Writing books allows Lou to share her passion with a broader audience to help people be more efficient. She has also taken learning to the web community through numerous webinars, online training, and the Project Management Peer Mentor virtual community.

As a sought-after international speaker, Lou blends humorous stories with her engaging on-the-ground experience to customize her presentation, facilitation, and teaching to the real problems of the people in the room. Encouraged by Lou's upbeat and practical style, every participant leaves with new enthusiasm and tools to improve their bottom line through their people. Her motto is *Lecture as a Last Resort.* You will be moving, laughing, participating, inspired, and challenged. Most important to Lou, you will learn.

Lou has spoken at over 300 conferences, including the ASTD International Conference, Society of Information Management (SIM), Training, American Museum Association, Nursing Educators, Career College Association, LOTU-Sphere, Project Management Institute, Project World, and at many corporate events, for over 20 years.

Lou writes a monthly e-zine, *Learning Flash*, with a loyal readership of over 20,000 people internationally. She tweets at @nolecture and you can easily find her and her adventures on Facebook. She has authored publicly available courses for Villanova University, Nielsen, Elluminate, Blackboard, Training Magazine Network, and ASTD. Her background includes an "expired" BS from Purdue University in Computer Science and an MS in Instructional Systems Technology from Indiana University. She is the original queen mother of the local "Wine and Whine" group in Indianapolis and past president of the local SIM chapter. Her business, Russell Martin & Associates, is a certified Women's Business Enterprise and a Project Management Institute education partner.

In her spare time, Lou learns from her husband and three daughters, loves turbo kick, and plays soccer. She only really knows one real joke. Find out more at www.lourussell.com or at www.russellmartin.com.

BIBLIOGRAPHY

Allen, David. (2002). *Getting Things Done: The Art of Stress Free Productivity*. London: Penguin.
   Personal Productivity. Controlling your to-do list.

Biech, Elaine. (1998). *The Business of Consulting*. San Francisco: Pfeiffer.

   We're all consultants, whether inside or out. Great tips for delivering results.

Bion, William. (1991). *Experiences in Groups*. Oxford: Routledge.

   A reprinted collection of Bion's research on group behavior.

Bridges, William, and Susan Bridges. (2009). *Managing Transitions: Making the Most of Change*.
   Cambridge, MA: Da Capo Lifelong Books.

   Original authors of the model I now use for scope diagrams, originally called "A Context Data
   Flow Diagram."

Brooks, Frederick P. (1995). *The Mythical Man Month*. Reading, MA: Addison-Wesley
   Professional.

   Research on how projects get late, and how adding people to a project is not a great idea.

Campbell, Joseph. (2008). *The Hero with a Thousand Faces*. Novato, CA: New World Library.

   The original collections of the Hero's Journey, recently reprinted.

Englund, Randy, and Alfonso Bucero. (2006). *Project Sponsorship: Achieving Management
   Commitment for Project Success*. San Francisco: Jossey-Bass.

   Great book on cultivating a strong relationship with the project sponsor.

Englund, Randy, and Robert Graham. (1997). *Creating an Environment for Successful Projects:
   The Quest to Manage Project Management*. San Francisco: Jossey-Bass.

   Powerful book on how to manage organizational project management.

Feldman, Jeff, and Karl Mulle. (2007). *Put Emotional Intelligence to Work*. Alexandria, VA: ASTD
   Press.

   Great, practical techniques for all the aspects of EQ.

Ford, D., and John D. Sterman. (2003). "The Liar's Club: Concealing Rework in Concurrent Development. Concurrent Engineering: Research and Applications" (white paper).
   Cambridge, MA: MIT Sloan Management.

   Original white paper about the impact of lying about status on project success.

Gardner, Howard. (2006). *Multiple Intelligences: New Horizons in Theory and Practice*. New York:
   Basic Books.

   The multidimensional aspects of intelligence; critical knowledge for designing learning.

Justice, Izzy. (2010). *EPowerment: Achieving Empowerment in the E World*. Bloomington, IN: IUniverse.

Recent research and thoughts about the impact of negative emotions on work productivity.

Knutson, Joan. (2001). *Project Management for Business Professionals: A Comprehensive Guide*. Hoboken, NJ: Wiley.

Want more detail? Here's the place to go.

Knutson, Joan. (2001). *Succeeding in Project-Driven Organizations: People, Processes and Politics*. Hoboken, NJ: Wiley.

Highly experienced, Joan knows what she's talking about on big, gnarly projects.

Neidigh, Chip. (2010). *The Catalyst OC Change Model*. Indianapolis, IN: CatalystOC.

Source for information about the CatalystOC Change Model and tool kit.

Project Management Institute. (2002). *A Guide to the PMBOK: Project Management Body of Knowledge*. Newton Square, PA: Project Management Institute.

Best practices of project management from www.pmi.org.

Russell, Lou. (2007). *10 Steps to Successful Project Management*. Alexandria, VA: ASTD Press.

Project management techniques to juggle small, highly matrixed projects.

Russell, Lou. (2005). *Leadership Training*. Alexandria, VA: ASTD Press.

A course in a book: teach leadership to self and others.

Russell, Lou. (2003). *Training Triage*. Alexandria, VA: ASTD Press.

Content and activities around various topics to deliver help quickly.

Russell, Lou. (2002). *The Accelerated Learning Fieldbook*. San Francisco: Jossey-Bass.

Learning theory in practice to build and deliver learning; includes a course development methodology.

Russell, Lou. (2000). *Project Management for Trainers*. Alexandria, VA: ASTD Press.

Project management specifically for learning professionals/trainers.

Russell, Lou, and Jeff Feldman. (2002). *IT Leadership Alchemy*. Upper Saddle River, NJ: Prentice Hall.

The ten competencies of a highly successful technical leader.

Senge, Peter, Art Kleiner, Charlotte Roberts, Rick Ross, and Bryan Smith. (1994). *The Fifth Discipline Fieldbook*. New York: Crown Business.

Techniques to grow organizational learning; including the Ladder of Inference.

Shackelford, Bill. (2002). *Project Managing E-Learning*. Alexandria, VA: ASTD Press.

The DPMR model I've developed applied to e-learning projects.

Stein, Stephen J., and Howard E. Book. (2006). *The EQ Edge*. San Francisco: Jossey-Bass.

Multiple techniques for emotional awareness, regulation, motivation, empathy, and social skills.

Valencic, Karen. (2011). *Spiral Impact: The Power to Get It Done with Grace*. Nevada City, CA: First Edition Design eBook.

Applying Spiral Impact focusing techniques during emotional times in projects.

Yourdon, Ed. (1988). *Modern Structured Analysis*. Upper Saddle River, NJ: Prentice Hall.

Original author of the model I now use for scope diagrams, originally called "A Context Data Flow Diagram."

INDEX

Problem-solving models: for determining milestones, 72; Systems Thinking and, 144–145

Processes: definition of, 8–10; examples of, 8–9; in updated to-do lists, 9

Processing styles, 29

Product development life cycle, 74*e*

Project Charter: audit of, 59, 60*s*; changes to, 67; creation of, 22–24, 59–61; definition of, 12; draft versus final, 62; importance of, 66; reuse of, 59–60; software for, 60–61

Project constraints: determining, during Define phase, 51–53; effects of, 51, 113–114; function of, 66; impact of change on, 102; of PMOs, 181

Project management: as career versus competency, 5; definition of, 14, 20; versus development process, 14–15; history of, 4–5; phases of, 10–13; versus project management software, 92; steps in, 11*e*; terminology of, 67; in various business sectors, 14–15

Project Management Body of Knowledge (PMBOK), 5; finalizing due dates in, 90; history of, 4

Project Management Institute, 4, 67

Project Management Office (PMO): benefits of, 178–179; creation of, 176; dashboard options in, 182–186; defined, 172, 176; defining roles in, 176; keys to success of, 175–176, 179; project plans that migrate to, 179–182; rationale for, 178–179; roles and processes of, 176–178; in small versus large organizations, 176–177; technology options for, 187–188

Project Management Professional certification, 4

Project management teams: in Agile approach, 74; autonomy of, 118; evolving nature of, 4; feedback to, 118–119; fragmentation of, 118; group dynamics in, 158–162; multitasking of, 19; for purpose of saving projects, 136; role of, 16–20; sources of stress for, 118–119; in Systems Thinking, 147

Project managers: accountability of, 67; in determining constraints, 51*e*; in determining project objectives, 40*e*; governance plans and, 57*e*; group dynamics and, 159–162; negotiation between stakeholders and, 39; PMO troubleshooting and, 184; project milestones and, 70*e*; as project sponsors, 16; response of, to change, 112–113; in risk mitigation, 44, 45*e*; role of, 16, 20, 172, 192; scope creep and, 28–29, 37; in scope diagrams, 32*e*, 33, 36; single versus multiple, 17; tips for success of, 191–193; typical story line of, 153–158; as writers of business objectives, 27

Project (Microsoft): description of, 93; for PMOs, 187

Project objectives: audits of, 66; categories of, 41*e*; definition of, 40; determining, 40–43; function of, 66; template for, 43*s*; writing of, 41–43. *See also* Business objectives/goals

Project plans: changes to, 66–67, 95; definition of, 67, 99; effects of change on, 112; function of, 94; that migrate to PMOs, 178–182; time management and, 65–66

Project portfolios, 9

Project schedules: definition of, 67; emailing of, 105

Project scope: constraints related to, 51–52; identification of, 28–39; inputs and outputs of, 29–31

Project sponsors: confusion about, 38; determining, 191–192; in determining constraints, 51*e*; in determining project objectives, 40*e*; governance plans and, 57*e*; initiation of change and, 113; lack of, 38; preproject checklist for, 17–18*e*; project inputs and outputs of, 30*e*; project managers as, 16; project milestones and, 70*e*; in risk mitigation, 45*e*; role of, 16–17, 20; in scope diagrams, 36; single versus multiple, 17, 38; as writers of business objectives, 27

Project status reports: communicating about, 104–109; creation of, 103–104; definition

Project status reports: (*continued*)
of, 102; emailing, 104–106; in project
kickoffs, 102–107; risk management and,
107

Project tasks: challenges in completing, 78,
81; definition of, 7, 82; effects of change
on, 112; effort and duration of, 9;
finalizing due dates for, 89–92;
identification of, 76–82; prioritizing, 15;
versus processes, 8–10; versus projects,
5–7; review of, 80*t*; stakeholders'
completion of, 88; in updated to-do lists,
9; updates of, 93. *See also* Task
dependencies

Projects: criteria for, 22; definition of, 7, 9;
versus processes, 8–10; recognizing, 22;
versus tasks, 5–7; in updated to-do lists, 9

Prototyping, 75

Q

Quality, of project, 51–52
Quick and Dirty Risk Assessment process,
44–50

R

Readiness, for organizational change, 164,
165–166*e*
Reflection, 148
Regulatory projects, 25–26
Reminders, 106
Reptilian-brain response, 123–124
Resentment, 161
Resilience, personal, 120–130
Resource dependencies, 86–88
Return on investment (ROI): challenges of
calculating, 26; definition of, 24
Review phase: blame-free atmosphere of,
138–139; causal loop diagrams in,
144–148; emotions in, 139–140; function
of, 136; groups involved in, 138; learning
histories in, 141–144; leveraging
knowledge gained in, 148–150; overview
of, 13, 136–137; in PMO creation,
179–182; prerequisites for, 139; standard
survey for, 141; steps in, 11*e*; timing of,
137–138

Risk: assessment of, 44–46; definition of, 44
Risk mitigation: in Define phase, 47–51;
effects of change on, 102, 113–114;
function of, 66; for PMOs, 181; status
updates and, 107
Road of Trials, 156–157
ROI. *See* Return on investment
Rules, in meetings, 139, 162*e*

S

Scope creep: cause of, 28–29; prevention of,
37
Scope diagrams: advantages of, 35–36;
challenges of, 38–39; communication
with, 35; completeness of, 37–38; creation
of, 31–35; effects of change on, 102;
example of, 32*e*; function of, 66; goal of,
29; graphics programs for, 61; importance
of, 192; influencing stakeholders while
creating, 39; people identified in, 36–38;
for PMOs, 180; processing style and, 29;
project milestones and, 71; symbols used
in, 33, 35; template for, 34*s*
Scrums, 74–75
Senge, P., 144
Shared beliefs, 159
SharePoint program, 61, 188
Skills instruction, 86
Social networking sites, 143
Software, project management: choices of,
93–95; description of, 92–93; lack of
project sponsor in, 38; for PMOs,
187–188; popular type of, 93; for project
charters, 60–61; versus project
management, 92; and skipping of Define
phase, 12; strength of, 12; time
management and, 93
Solid lines, in scope diagrams, 33
Spiral Impact, 128
Staff reductions, iv
Stakeholders: completion of tasks by, 88; in
determining constraints, 51*e*; in
determining project objectives, 40*e*;
effects of change on, 111, 112; emailing
status reports to, 104–106; finalizing due
dates and, 91–92; governance plans and,

57e; increased number of, 19; obtaining consensus among, 39; as participants in Review phase, 137–138; plan for communicating with, 53–56; project inputs and outputs of, 29–31; project milestones and, 70e, 71; as resource dependencies, 88; response of, to change, 99; in risk mitigation, 44, 45e, 50–51; role of, 19, 20; scope creep and, 28–29; in scope diagrams, 32e, 33, 36, 37; system as, 39–40; task dependencies and, 84–86; task identification and, 81, 82e; writing of business objectives and, 27–28

Standard Surveys, 141, 142e

Status reports. *See* Project status reports

Stermann, J., 110

Story of Origin, 153–158, 159s

Strategic level, of change management, 163e, 164

Stress: awareness of, 120, 126–127; benefits of, 124; building resiliency to, 120–130; control of project and, 101; sources of, 118–119

Successful projects: criteria for, 44; importance of communication to, 3; key to, 144

Surveys, in Review phase, 139–148

Survival mode, 123

Systems Thinking, 144–148

T

Tactical level, of change management, 163e, 164

Tagline, project, 167s

Task dependencies: definition of, 82; determining, in Plan phase, 82–86; example of, 84e; redundancy in, 85e. *See also* Project tasks

Task owners, assignment of, 87s, 92

Tasks. *See* Project tasks

Technology: addition of, during project, 137; effects of, on multitasking, iv; for PMOs, 187–188

Time constraints: determining, 51–52; Review phase and, 137–138

Time management: demands of email in, 4; effects of change on, 112; effort and duration in, 9; finalizing due dates and, 89–92; importance of project plans, 65–66; software and, 93; steps to improve, 10

To-do lists: daily updates to, 9–10; employee frustrations and, 5–6; projects versus tasks on, 6–7

Towers Perrin, 2

Training classes, 72e

Transitions, 114–116

Trust, 118

U

Uhl, T., 184

V

Valencic, K., 127

Velocity, 74

Vision, 162

W

Wass, D. L., 129

Waterfall methodologies, 73

Webinars, 148

Work Breakdown Structure (WBS): description of, 76; example of, 79e; template for, 80s

Workload: forces affecting, iv; unrealistic number of projects in, 152

Workshop development: development processes of, 14; objectives of, 41–42; for Review phase, 138